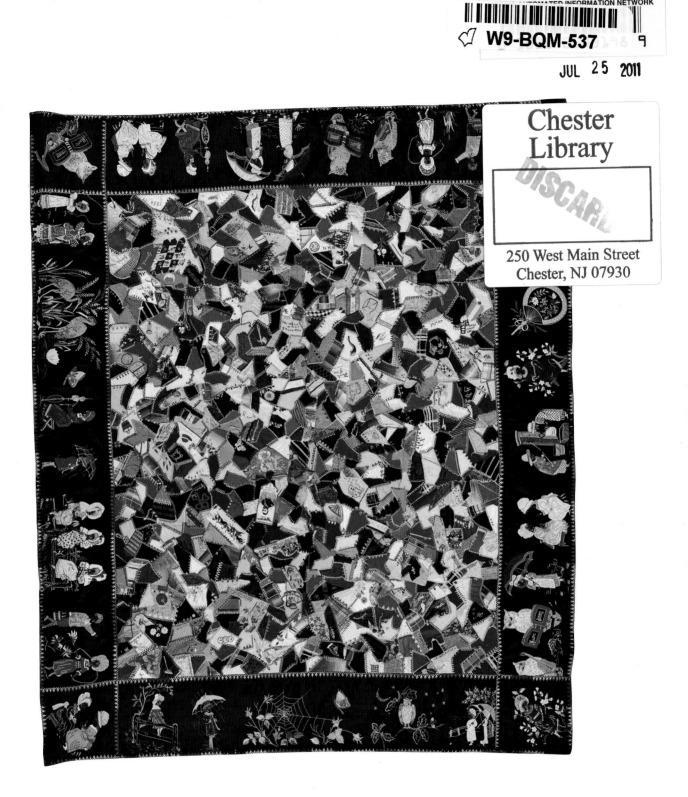

"Our lives are patchwork, and it depends on us a good deal how the bright and dark bits get put together so that the whole is neat, pretty, and useful when it is done . . . Every task, no matter how small or homely, that gets well and cheerfully done, is a fine thing; and the sooner we learn to use up the dark and bright bits (the pleasures and pains, the cares and duties) into a cheerful, useful life, the sooner we become real comforters."

—Louisa M. Alcott, "Patty's Patchwork," *Aunt Jo's Scrap-Bag*

CRAZY QUILTS

History ◆ Techniques ◆ Embroidery Motifs

Cindy Brick

Foreword by Nancy Kirk, Crazy Quilt Society founder

Voyageur Press

First published in 2008 by Voyageur Press, an imprint of MBI Publishing Company LLC, Galtier Plaza, Suite 200, 380 Jackson Street, St. Paul, MN 55101 USA

MBI Publishing Company titles are also available at discounts in bulk quantity for industrial or sales-promotional use. For details write to Special Sales Manager at MBI Publishing Company, Galtier Plaza, Suite 200, 380 Jackson Street, St. Paul, MN 55101 USA

Editors: Margret Aldrich and Amy Rost
Designer: Sara Holle

Printed in China

On the front cover:
Fringed Crazy detail. See page 16 to view full quilt. (Minnesota Historical Society)

Frontispiece:
Victorian Crazy | Date: ca. 1886 | Maker: Unknown | Size: 76" x 65"
This glorious Crazy quilt is made from silks and velvets, and it includes an unusual border of Kate Greenaway–influenced figures. (Fenimore Art Museum, Cooperstown, New York. Photograph by Richard Walker.)

On the dedication page:
An early 1900s trompe l'oeil postcard (woman at left), complemented by a nineteenth-century man with silk checkered tie. (No doubt the tie scraps went into a Crazy quilt!)

On the contents page:
A mix of nineteenth- and twentieth-century Crazy ephemera, including fabric and pattern catalogs, cigarette silks, trade cards, ribbons, and more. The late nineteenth century, especially, had an incredible amount of Crazy-related items for resale and giveaway. (Photograph by Teressa Mahoney, Forever Yours Photography)

On the back cover:
Main, Victorian Crazy (Fenimore Art Museum, Cooperstown, New York. Photograph by Richard Walker.)
Inset, trade card, ca. 1886.

Library of Congress Cataloging-in-Publication Data

Brick, Cindy.
Crazy quilts : history, techniques, embroidery motifs / by Cindy Brick.
p. cm.
ISBN-13: 978-0-7603-3237-5 (hardbound w/ jacket)
1. Patchwork—Patterns. 2. Embroidery—Patterns. 3. Crazy quilts—United States—History. I. Title.
TT835.B6993 2008
746.46'041—dc22
2007030862

DEDICATION

For Nancy Kirk, my dear, Crazy friend.
And for David. Always David.

CONTENTS

ACKNOWLEDGMENTS

This book has been in the making for so many years. And over that time, many other people's ideas and contributions have influenced my own. I owe much to the great scholars of Crazy history, especially Virginia Gunn. A *Quilter's Newsletter* editorial assignment and Penny McMorris's thought-provoking book *Crazy Quilts* started me on this road; Nancy Kirk from the Crazy Quilt Society was the one to point out the signposts and set the pace. Dee Stark has challenged and inspired my thoughts on the origins and meanings. And some of the greatest Crazy quilters, restorers, and teachers have influenced my own work, including Leslie Levison, Betty Pillsbury, Chris Dabbs, Camille Cognac, and Judith Baker Montano.

I am grateful for the quilt-loving friends I've made over the years, including the editors and artists at *Quilter's Newsletter* and *McCall's Quilting*. I am proud to call them friends and colleagues. Thanks especially to Barbara, Vivian, Jan and Beth, Sandee, Ellie, and to Barbara Smith, as well. I appreciate the thoughts, ideas, and encouragement of fellow appraisers, especially Newbie Richardson, Kathy Kansier, Sally Ambrose, Carol Pratt, Vivien Sayre, and dear Teddy Pruett, whose style is always just a little bit . . . well, you know. A thankful nod to Merikay Waldvogel, who wouldn't take a casual answer, but forced me to *think*

about it. And love to Constance Mullans for her thoughtful questions and encouragement.

There are also the many dear friends gained through the Crazy Quilt Society, the Quilt Restoration Society, and the Quilt Heritage Listserv (QHL), including Mary Waller, Kris and John Driessen, Bill and Nancy Kirk (Bill now gone, but never forgotten), Joan Stevens, Gloria Hall, Carolyn Ducey, Mary Ghormley, Sandy Bonsib, Xenia Cord, and others. They made me think things through and provided many a moment of pure joy. This Crazy life wouldn't be the same without any of you in it.

Thank you also to the many institutions and collectors who loaned their quilts to be shared in this book. Their kindness and generosity is much appreciated. Please note that all quilt dimensions given are approximate. All paper ephemera and memorabilia come from the collection of the author, unless otherwise indicated.

Thank you to my long-suffering and patient editors at Voyageur Press, Margret Aldrich and Amy Rost; see, I made it! Thanks also to my designer Sara Holle.

But most of all, I could not do this without my family, who have put up with Mom in near-permanent newsletter mode and stuff everywhere for years. Thanks, David, Jess, and Angel. The fourth member of this family will always love you.

AUTHOR'S NOTE

In Jane Austen's *Persuasion*, one of the characters says, "I do not think I ever opened a book in my life which had not something to say upon woman's inconstancy. Songs and proverbs all talk of woman's fickleness. But . . . *these were all written by men*" [emphasis mine].

Anyone who does quilt and textile research struggles with the same problem. For hundreds of years, patchwork and other forms of needlework were considered in the realm of women. These needle arts were genteel and useful, of course, but hardly important enough for writers—the majority of whom were male—to write about.

Today's researcher will find various forms of needlework described, including patterns. Needlework advertisements appeared regularly in magazines designed for women, which began to be published in the 1820s and 1830s. (With the publication of these magazines, the number of women writers and editors increased, although they still tended to take the genteel viewpoint, rather than the honest one.) However, their instructions were not always practical—or accurate. This "genteel" viewpoint can make it difficult to follow the trail of a particular quilt style. Why is a particular style mentioned one year, but rarely two, five, or even ten years later?

Part of the answer is that all craft forms follow a cyclical pattern. Needlework people love trends. Knitting, crochet, and other yarn-based crafts are seeing an upturn in popularity. As of this writing, many quilters use (and love) hand-dyed batiks—a fabric choice that was confined largely to experimenters and art quilters two decades ago. Give life five years or so, and we'll see something else emerge.

Whether we like to admit it or not, we are heavily influenced by the world we live in. Politics, wars, religion, natural disasters, current events—these all work together to shape our views and opinions. They also affect quilters' choices of pattern and design and give our work life and importance. A quilt magazine may not always mention a war in Iraq or Afghanistan, but it is impossible to ignore patterns featuring patriotic messages or color schemes. Yesterday's needle artists had the same passions and fervent beliefs, the same love for their family and their home.

This history, therefore, considers not only what was being made and when—but also *why*.

FOREWORD

Crazy quilts are addictive, and once you get hooked they become a lifetime passion. They are full of surprises. I've seen something new in every Crazy quilt I've ever looked at—a new stitch combination, a new embellishment motif, a new fabric, a new painting technique, some new ribbonwork, a new historic ribbon—the list goes on and on.

Cindy Brick learned just how addictive these oddball creatures of the quilting world can be about ten years ago. She had been aware of them earlier, but when a job change allowed her time to take over the editor's position for the Crazy Quilt Society newsletter, she jumped in with enthusiasm, but without realizing what a consuming passion Crazies would become.

Over the years, her exploration of the history of Crazy quilting has led her to new theories about the origins of the art form, which are mysteries that have long intrigued all of us who love these unique quilts.

If you are new to Crazy quilting, as a collector, a scholar, or a quilter, you are embarking on a never-boring, never-ending journey with wonderful visual adventures around every corner. As you turn the pages of this "common sense" history of Crazy quilts, you will meet quilters who broke all the rules of quilting. They invented a form of abstract art a generation before the painters who became famous for it.

If you have been in love with Crazy quilts for years or decades, you will see them anew as Cindy explores the development of the form over time. You'll find something new in every quilt—look closely. As a quilter, you will find techniques to adapt in your quilts today. As a collector, you'll see great examples of the breadth and depth of the field.

As I have studied Crazy quilts over the years, I've found parallels in other art forms. Crazy quilts are to patchwork quilts what jazz is to a symphony. Jazz is improvisational,

Crazy-patched trade card, one of a series, ca. 1886.

but works within a structure. The final result is most noticeable for the individual touches the artist brings to the underlying foundation of the melody, rhythm, and key.

Similarly, Crazy quilts build on a foundation, use a structure of blocks or wholecloth style, and may borrow elements of "sane" quilts, like sashing and borders. But within those most basic elements of structure the artist takes off on a flight of fancy, adding stitches, embellishments, ribbons, charms, buttons, fabrics, yarns—even animals, toys, and more.

I always tell my beginning Crazy-quilt students that I have three rules for Crazy quilting:

There are no rules.

Always underlap velvets (the opposite of overlap).

Crazy quilts are the one thing in life where more is more. In almost all other aspects of our lives, less is more—in design, architecture, eating—we are advised "moderation in all things." Crazy quilts are the exception. They get better the more you add, and a crazy quilt is only done when you can't stand working on it anymore.

Cindy Brick has learned these lessons well. Now she is sharing a decade of study and research with all of us. Enjoy!

Nancy Kirk
The Crazy Quilt Society

Nancy Kirk is a quilt historian, appraiser, and restorer. She lectures and teaches nationally on Crazy quilting, quilt history, and quilt restoration. She has produced two DVD sets on quilt restoration, another on dating fabrics, and the books Collecting Antique Quilts *and* Taking Care of Grandma's Quilt. *She and her late husband, Bill, started The Kirk Collection in 1987 dealing in antique quilts and antique fabrics. Nancy serves as president of the Quilt Heritage Foundation, which sponsors the Quilt Preservation Society and the Crazy Quilt Society (www.crazyquilt.com).*

Victorian Crazy | Date: ca. 1885 | Maker: Unknown, except photograph | Size: 62 ½" x 52"

We know what the maker of this lovely piece looks like, thanks to her daguerreotype. The quilt was purchased in Oxford, Nebraska— but nothing else is known, not even the maker's name. (Collection of Mary Ghormley. Photograph by Teressa Mahoney, Forever Yours Photography.)

THE HISTORY OF THE CRAZY QUILT

In the 1880s, a new form of needlework flashed across American books, magazines, and advertising. Within a few short years, this concoction filled parlors and bed-sitting rooms across the country, from the lambrequins that framed the windows to the picture frames and mantelpiece covers—yes, beds and couches, too.

That style was the Crazy quilt. Embroidered on every seam (and more), filled with vivid, random shapes and intriguing images, the Crazy became the epitome of elegance. *Webster's New World Dictionary* defines a "crazy quilt" as "a quilt made of pieces of cloth of various colors and irregular shapes and sizes." Other forms of patchwork rely on tidy patches marching across the quilt, evenly spaced and neatly matched. But the Crazy revels in irregular bits and pieces strewn in seemingly disorganized fashion. The fabrics can be silks, wools, cottons, artificial fibers, or even a mix. These fabrics are pieced, appliquéd, and otherwise fitted on a fabric background for the most popular method. But Crazies can also be pieced in other ways, including no fabric foundation at all!

The oldest Crazies were generally pieced and embellished by hand, though machines contributed their share of beautiful work, both for home techniques and commercial embellishments. Today's Crazies may be completely stitched by hand, completely by machine, or both. But whatever its makeup, construction, or style, the Crazy is a perfect starting point for exploration and creation. One 1884 book, *Crazy Patchwork*, announced, "No species of fancy-work yet invented, has ever given more scope for the exercise of artistic ability and real originality; hence, the secret of its wonderful popularity. It is probable that it will exercise its fascinations for years to come."

All gushing aside, that prediction has come true. Of all the varied styles that patchwork boasts over the centuries, the Crazy quilt is one of the most unusual. Its very name, *Crazy*, could mean insane—or clever. Some critics say that Crazies are not a true patchwork style. Rose Wilder Lane, in her 1963 classic *Woman's Day Book of American Needlework*, snorted, "I wouldn't throw one away, but I would not call it patchwork. True patchwork is designed; it has meaning in every line."

Crazy patches are stitched in place just as neatly as their more controlled siblings, but their seam lines are often knowingly splashed with lavish threads and glistening beads. Ribbons, cigarette and tobacco silks (silk-screened images of every sort of theme and motif imaginable, tucked in packages of cigarettes and cigars), photo transfers, even images of pretty girls,

Victorian Crazy | Date: ca. 1885 | Maker: Cordelia Teachout | Size: 77" x 64"

Family history holds that two dressmaker sisters from Farmington, Minnesota, Anna and Orena Teachout, stitched this quilt, though Cordelia Teachout is registered as its maker. The piece includes an 1885 Minnesota State Fair ribbon and a wide variety of silks, including velvet, taffeta, and ribbons with embroidery trim. (Minnesota Historical Society)

printed on hat linings that were frugally cut out and recycled, are nudged into place on the surface. Painted and embroidered flowers, pictures of children, odd little figures, letters, dates, even musical scores fill each open spot. Traditional quilts sometimes follow the pristine "less is more" philosophy. But for Crazies, more is never enough.

Today, many Crazy quilts, like their Victorian-era ancestors, are stitched from mostly fancy fabrics: velvets, satins, brocades, and such. Silk is most popular on the fiber list; wool and synthetics are next, but cottons, especially textures and batiks, are in favor, as well. Sometimes the patchwork squares, strips, triangles, or rectangles may be sashed, or put together in long vertical or horizontal strips. More often they're simply joined to make a larger top that acts visually as one piece. Borders and binding—sometimes embroidered and trimmed, sometimes not—often complete the quilt. In Victorian times, it was popular to edge the finished quilt with a heavy cording, also known as gimp, or with wide borders of handmade lace.

ORIGINS OF THE CRAZY STYLE

The earliest so-called Crazy quilt may not have been meant for a bed at all, but made as a garment. Venice's carnival, said to have originated in 1162, and its *commedia dell'arte* includes Harlequin, a magical character dressed in a "particolored," or colorful, patched costume; the patches could be remnants of other, richer costumes. Sometimes the colors on Harlequin's clothes are evenly divided—an arm of one color, a leg of another—but on other occasions he appears in a suit of basted-together patches that look much like Crazy patchwork. Quilt historian Camille Cognac cites the Harlequin's costume as one of the earliest appearances of the Crazy patchwork style. (Today, we usually see him in a tight-fitting leotard of large-scale triangles, sometimes with jingling cap.)

Harlequin has plenty of company in the traditional fool or jester of the Middle Ages and Renaissance, whose costume was much the same. These individuals (who sometimes had mental and/or physical handicaps) wore costumes featuring bits and pieces of various fabrics, often accented by

A woman wears a kimono-style dress in this 1886 illustration from Godey's Lady's Book.

bells and "asses' ears." Fools were fixtures of royal and aristocratic households, amusing and shocking the audiences by their droll words and odd ways. Perhaps the fool's Crazy-style outfit was a reflection of his supposedly "crazy" manner.

In the sixteenth century, another, much more sophisticated group would don Crazy-patched clothing on occasion: Japanese nobility. Their choice of clothing—kimonos of silk and wool that were often hand painted and embroidered—communicated not only their political and family ties, but also their taste in flora and fauna. At least one sixteenth-century kimonos-style outer garment, still existing today, includes uneven, Crazy-style patchwork joined together in long strips. Pieced from gold and silver silk brocades and damask, it was used by Uesugi Kenshin about 1560.

Fringed Crazy | Date: ca. 1920 | Maker: Dora Timm | Size: 88" x 87"

Colorful embroidered flowers, leaves, and buds are scattered over the surface of this charming Crazy, and two sides of the quilt feature blackish-blue fringe. (Minnesota Historical Society)

Crazy patchwork for costumes and dresses was surprisingly popular—but not with the amount of leg the girl is showing in this 1880s photo!

"Butterfly Magic," a modern-day Crazy-pieced ball gown, made by Judith Baker Montano for her daughter, Madeleine Montano, "because she is truly a butterfly!" Made of silk and satins, the bustier is heavily embroidered. (Photograph courtesy of the quiltmaker)

EARLY AMERICAN CRAZY STYLE

Some suggest that what we know today as the Crazy-patched style was really a method of necessity. For thousands of years, only those well-off could afford to buy fabric ready-made; others wove their own fabric or went without. It would make no sense for someone to go to the trouble of weaving yardage, then cut it up for no other reason than decoration. It would make sense, though, to patch—and continue patching—an item of clothing to keep it in gainful use. Eventually, multipatched clothing and bedcoverings would come to resemble Crazy patchwork. These pieces would probably be mostly wool. Although linen was probably used as well, it would have most likely been reserved for larger patches.

(Stitchers who work with linen know that it tends to fray, especially when used in smaller patches.) Early quilts tended to be one large piece, or whole cloth *calimancos* (from the Persian word for "calico"). They were generally made with imported wool on top, home-woven wool or linen as the backing, and wool batting in between. They were heavily quilted in a variety of designs to help hold the batting in place. Any holes or rips in that expansive surface would need a patch, then another, and so on.

In *Romance of the Patchwork Quilt*, a comprehensive book of more than one thousand patterns, Carrie A. Hall awards pride of place to a square with uneven patches sewn sparingly across it. Her description of it says, "This is a sample of original

Two women machine-sew a crazy-patched quilt in this 1890s hand-colored photograph. (Fred Hulstrand History in Pictures Collection, NDIRS-NDSU, Fargo)

These 1901 postcards come from the Julius Bier series "Simple Life." Note the girl's patchwork dress.

American patchwork as conceived by our early Colonial mothers. With the frugality necessary in the early days of our country, they cut from worn and discarded woolen clothing the patches of material yet intact and considered useful, and sewed them together 'crazy fashion' and with a back and padding or interlining . . . this is an all-over pattern." Averil Colby, another well-respected quilt historian, does not mention Crazy patchwork specifically in her book *Patchwork Quilts*, but she wryly mentions that "[a] characteristic of English traditional patchwork during its best period from about 1780 until 1830—discounting the excellence of pattern and colour—was the economy in materials, time and work given to it."

According to quilt historians of the early twentieth century, Crazy quilts made a very early appearance in the American colonies, possibly sometime in the seventeenth century. Penny McMorris, author of *Crazy Quilts*, the first modern reference book devoted entirely to the Crazy style, says, "The crazy quilt has become known as the oldest American quilt pattern." She credits Ruth Finley, one of quilting's earliest historians, with the theory that Crazies originated in colonial America. Finley's 1929 book, *Old Patchwork Quilts and the Women Who Made Them*, says, "In Colonial days, when every finger's wrapping of cloth was brought from Europe in sailing vessels at almost prohibitive cost, each scrap left from the cutting of clothing was worth as much as its equivalent in the garment itself. Thus the 'Crazy Patch,' fitted irregularly together so that not a thread of the valuable material was wasted, came into being."

Elizabeth Wells Robertson echoes Finley's assertion in her own 1948 book, *American Quilts*. Robertson, however, attributes the origin of Crazies to a slightly different dilemma—not how to put every scrap of new fabric to good use, but how to salvage old but still-good fabrics:

> Soon the women [of the early colonies] found that they did not have nearly enough clothes and bedding, nor sufficient quantities of materials with which to make quilts. Therefore, as clothing wore out they cut away the worn parts

and saved every tiny piece that would be useful in making coverings for their beds. From the foregoing, we can readily see how the first quilt, the Crazy Quilt came into being.

Though other early twentieth-century historians agreed with Robertson, modern quilt historians have dismissed this idea. Lynne Z. Bassett points out in *Northern Comfort: New England's Early Quilts 1780–1850*:

> The romantic historians of the late nineteenth and early twentieth centuries have created an enduringly sentimental vision of early New England quilting. From the beginning of settlement, they assumed, New England women could be found frugally piecing quilts from bits of leftover cloth . . . This is an attractive vision but not an accurate one.
>
> Quilts of any kind were very rare in New England in the seventeenth and early eighteenth centuries, and it is unlikely that New England women were making quilts in any number until at least the 1750s. All of the evidence indicates that the great majority of quilts on early American beds during this period were expensive imported items, a few from India but most of them from England, where they were commercially made by the upholstery trade.

We know very little about actual quilts made in colonial days. No documented seventeenth-century quilts have been found in America—yet—although a very few exist in other countries, including England and Italy. (A good sampling of these very early European pieces is shown in Colby's *Patchwork Quilts*.) Quilts are occasionally listed in American estate inventories from that time, including a "flock bed quilt" owned by Samuel Fuller of Plymouth Colony in 1633. (*Flock* referred to the quilt's stuffing of wool or chopped-up fabrics, notes Bassett.) But Sally Garoutte, in her essay "Early Colonial Quilts in a Bedding Context," points out that references to quilts in colonial records "were few and far between."

"They were found in the households of well-to-do people, usually merchant-importers. They were almost certainly imported rather than home-made," she says, adding, "The bedding of the 17th century consisted primarily of woolen blankets, woolen bed rugs, and coverlets—which were some-times woolen and sometimes linen." Garoutte's sources were probate inventories and wills from Providence, Rhode Island; the Plymouth colony; New Hampshire; and Hartford, Connecticut—doc-uments from as early as 1631 to as late as 1749.

The reasons for this general lack of quilts are straightforward, according to Susan Jenkins and Linda Seward:

> Despite strong English quilting traditions, in pre-Revolutionary America conditions were generally unfavorable for quiltmaking. Houses were small, cramped and dirty. Imported mate-rials were scarce and expensive and homespun fabric was mostly used for other household items rather than for quilted bedcovers. In addition, the commercial manufacture of cloth was strictly prohibited, although fabric, flax, seed and sheep were smuggled into the country . . . [E]xamination of probate inventories and wills from New England and the Eastern coastal regions confirms that quilts were "few and far between."

Traditional Crazy patchwork, especially that done during the Victorian period, often consists of a fabric background with scraps appliquéd or basted on top. Penny McMorris cites this popular method as further proof that the Crazy's origins are not colo-nial, saying, "*foundation fabric is a necessary part of the quilt top as long as the edges of the fabric scraps are irregu-larly shaped*" (italics mine). Since this patchwork method requires large pieces of backing to use even the smallest scraps, and fabric yardage was expensive and hard to obtain in the American colonies, McMorris argues that "the earliest American quilts were not crazy quilts, requiring additional fabric for foundation pieces, but scrap quilts made of squares, strips, or rectangles that could be pieced together without an additional fabric backing."

We know that quilts existed and were in use in seventeenth- and early eighteenth-century America, but no historical sources describe anything remotely like the "irregular shapes and sizes" of Crazy patch-work. The door seems to have slammed shut on the idea of an early American Crazy quilt.

Or has it?

The Case for an Early American Crazy

Modern quilt historians have tended to reject the idea of a colonial-era Crazy, along with the early twentieth-century historians, such as Hall, Finley, and Robertson, who were its proponents. These lat-ter historians are alleged to have been too quick to jump to conclusions, too anecdotal. Hall and compa-ny were not museum-trained and, by and large, not that well educated. Their stories were good for a cozy read, but not meant to be taken seriously. Therefore, any conclusions they drew about any aspect of quilting and needlework are suspect. Or so their detractors say.

Before today's readers also dismiss these sources, however, some points need to be considered.

Finley and her fellow historians could inter-view people with direct ties to the time periods in question. Many of the early twentieth-century histo-rians began their research decades before their books and articles were published. And their sources could easily have been elderly individuals passing along information they received directly from parents or other relatives who lived in colonial times. (In some instances, this was definitely the case.) Today, our direct information sources don't date much before the 1930s and 1940s, and that generation is dying out quickly. Time stands still for no one—quilt researchers included.

The early twentieth-century historians had access to earlier archives and collections that, in some cases at least, were more complete than we have today. We may have the Internet and micro-fiche to make our work easier, but many primary sources have been subject to decades of time, neglect, and catastrophes. Certain print sources, such as nineteenth-century magazines like *Godey's Lady's Book* and *Peterson's Magazine*, are fairly well docu-mented, but other old periodicals, newspapers, and books, especially those stored in rural areas, have not fared as well. Many old quilts simply have not sur-vived to the present day, either, due to carelessness

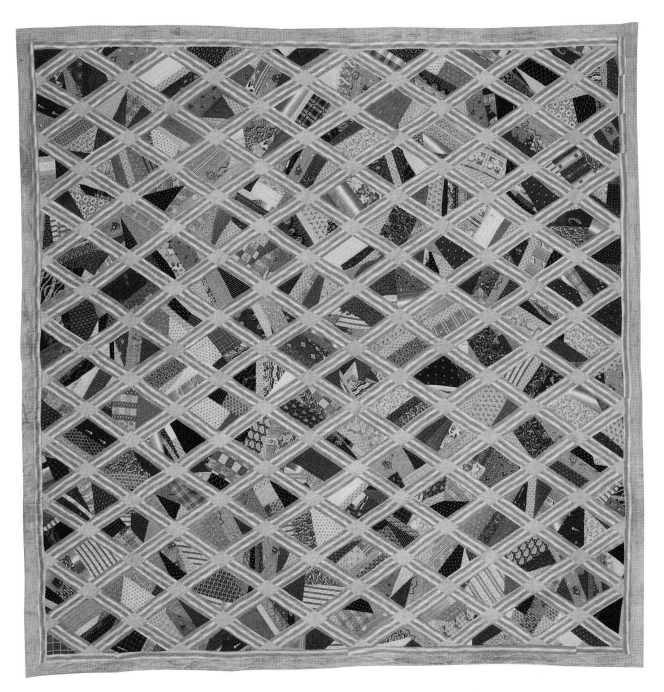

Contained Crazy with Cross of St. Andrew setting | Date: ca. 1860
| Maker: Unknown, Pennsylvania | Size: 84" x 84"
*When presented diagonally, the unique sashed setting of this cotton Contained
Crazy is called Cross of St. Andrew. The example shown here is pieced in the
popular ombre or "rainbow" prints of the 1850s; a similar quilt in sampler form was
included in Shelly Zegart's* American Quilt Collection: Antique Quilt
Masterpieces. *(Collection of the author. Photographs by Mellisa Karlin Mahoney,
courtesy of* Quilter's Newsletter.)

and natural disasters. But the early historians would have viewed these items in their prime.

Finley and company were not only historians, but often practicing quiltmakers as well. They understood earlier quilting and patchwork styles, methods, and techniques because they often made their own versions. Even Florence Peto, an early quilt historian who collected fabrics and quilts, made at least one reproduction quilt in the old styles she loved. Carrie Hall decided to make one block of every pattern she came across; after more than a thousand, she gave up the effort. Even those who were not actively sewing—Marie Webster comes to mind—often designed patterns.

Finally, these early chroniclers were anecdotal—and proud of it. They recognized the power of a good story to preserve and pass on information to future generations. True, that story may change over the years of telling and retelling. Someone once said that every story has an element of truth—it's just up to us to figure out how much.

AMERICA'S OLDEST DATED CRAZY QUILT?

Quilts done in the uneven patchwork characterized as Crazy appear early in the nineteenth century, long before the Crazy reached its heyday between 1875 and 1900. Most of these quilts are undated; their age is established by the materials used to make them, as well as their size, construction, and quilting styles. (Professionals such as museum curators and appraisers have used this method of evaluation for centuries.)

One piece, however, has a provenance that describes its creation. In 1996 the Maryland Historical Society acquired the "Kaleidoscope" quilt during an auction by the Fitzhughs, a Quaker family. The wife and mother, Martha Ellicott Tyson, was one of seven children born to George and Elizabeth Brooke Ellicott, a well-known milling family who lived in Ellicott Mills, Maryland. Appraisers Bunnie Jordan and Hazel Carter, whose experience stretches for decades, attended the Fitzhugh auction and were the first to recognize the quilt's connection to Crazy patchwork. They examined the quilt closely and confirmed its fabrics were from 1835 or earlier. I examined the quilt in 2002 and saw no fabrics, thread, construction, or quilting methods that would conflict with a pre-1840 date. It has no embroidery, no fancy stitching, but the surface of the top is pieced from a wide variety of early cotton chintzes, prints, and weaves. It has a wide chintz border, and its plain cotton backing features the date 1839 cross-stitched in red thread on one side.

The 110- by 115-inch quilt was made by combining forty-two patchwork squares, each

Note the early chintz and madder (pinkish-red) prints featured in this quilt. The "little calico man . . . made by my sister Anne" is the only motif that stands out; there may be some random appliquéd patches. (Photographs by the author)

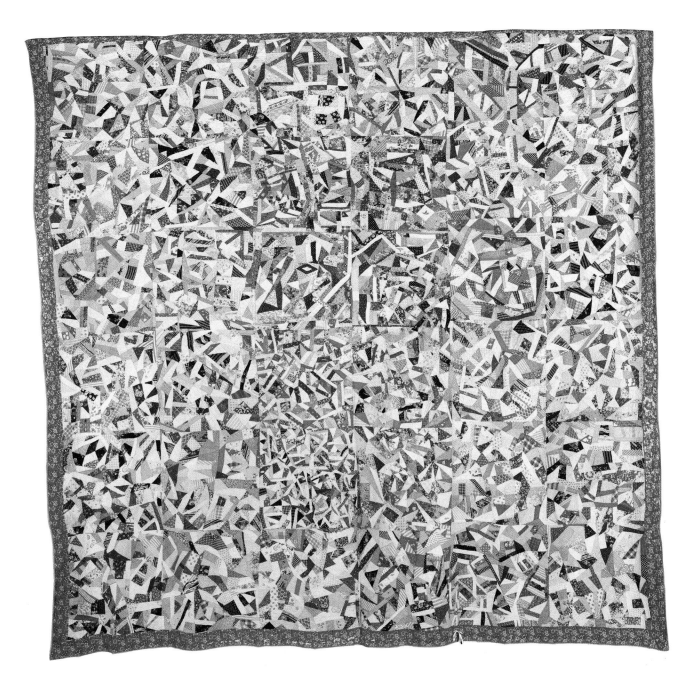

"**Kaleidoscope**" | Date: 1839 | Maker: Probably Martha
Ellicott Tyson | Size: 110" x 115"
*This fragile quilt was pieced in blocks—but not on a fabric
foundation. A wide variety of cotton chintzes, plaids, stripes, and
other fabrics, ranging from the 1830s to decades earlier, gives the
quilt texture and interest overall. The 1839 date is cross-stitched on
the backing fabric. (Maryland Historical Society)*

RIGHT: *The author studied the 1839 Kaleidoscope quilt in the
Maryland Historical Society's examination room. (Photograph by
the author)*

23

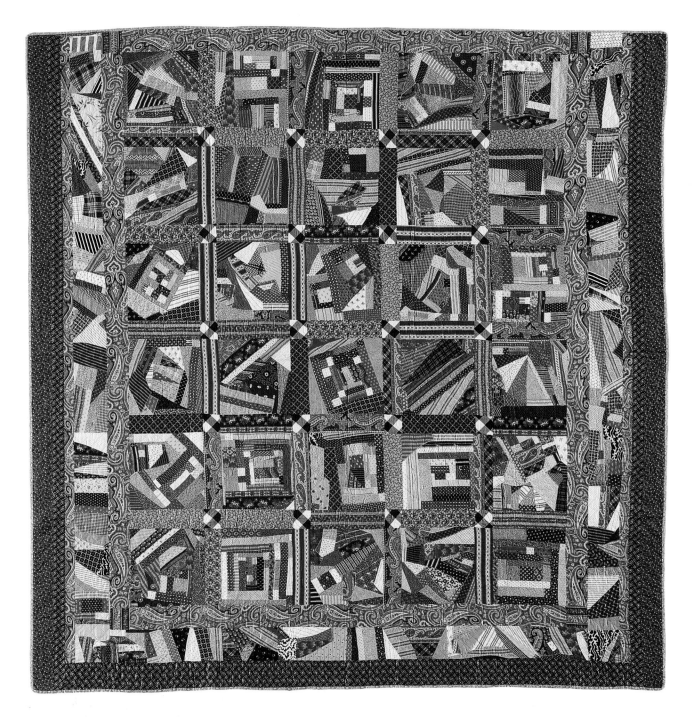

Contained Crazy | Date: ca. 1880 | Maker: Unknown | Size: 80" x 80"

Early cotton Crazies are far more common in the Pennsylvania region than any other, whether from the 1880s, like this square quilt, or earlier. The sampler pieced blocks and varied sashing feature bright "Lancaster blues," double pinks, madder browns, and manganese "Hershey" browns. (Los Angeles County Museum of Art)

approximately 17 by 17 inches, in seven rows of six. The squares are mostly pieced, but contain some calico appliqué, as well. They are joined without sashing, and there is a red calico border around them all.

Although backed by muslin, the quilt has no batting. (Possibly it was meant to be a lightweight summer spread.) It is quilted in a close overall pattern of diamonds and bound with half-inch-wide beige-and-blue-striped twill tape.

The Maryland Kaleidoscope's size, which seems so large today, was not uncommon to that time period. In fact, one of the hallmarks of a pre-1850s quilt is its larger size—usually 90 inches or more—and its shape—square or nearly square. The Maryland Kaleidoscope's quilting and binding are also familiar to the time period; many quilts were quilted with a close overall pattern to keep the unbonded cotton battings from shifting and separating. Binding with twill tape was a hallmark of an earlier East Coast quilt.

Ironically, the Maryland Kaleidoscope's cross-stitched date—the one item that would seem to prove its provenance more than anything else—brings up more questions than it satisfies. The cross-stitching is very similar to that used to mark linens for housekeeping inventories. Could the Fitzhughs have reused an old sheet to finish their quilt? The date's positioning is puzzling, too. Instead of appearing on a corner, as was common, it is a good ways from the edge of the quilt.

One of the most intriguing parts to this date puzzle is a 1913 note by Lucy Tyson Fitzhugh of Baltimore County, Maryland. According to Lucy, who would have been five at the time of the quilt's making, the top was pieced by her mother, Martha Ellicott Tyson, and Lucy's three older sisters. Lucy records that the Kaleidoscope, "made of small calico scraps out of the rag bags," was pieced during the time the family lived in Jericho Mills, Maryland, in 1838. "Grandmother had it quilted at Ellicott Mills [Maryland]," Lucy wrote, adding that her grandmother put "a white mark on the red border to locate where a little calico man is—he was made by my sister Anne." Interestingly, the "little calico man" is pieced, not appliquéd, into the quilt top.

This level of documentation is unusual for any quilt, but especially for one from the early nineteenth century, and strengthens the Crazy's claim to a pre-1850s origin. But there are some problems.

First, the backing date is one year earlier than Lucy's recollections. If the cross-stitching was meant to cement the date of the quilt, something is wrong. Also, three sets of initials are embroidered on the quilt top, but they match those of Lucy's aunt, Elizabeth Ellicott Lea, and her two daughters. Did they really stitch the quilt, or did they add their initials when the top was quilted in Ellicott Mills?

Second, one of the most telling arguments for the Maryland Kaleidoscope having been made in 1839 is its construction. Unlike its Victorian brothers and sisters, the quilt was not made of fabric scraps appliquéd to a larger background; *there is no fabric background foundation at all.* Instead, the scraps are stitched and fitted directly to each other, much like pieces in a picture puzzle. Uneven and irregular patchwork can be done without a fabric foundation, but this is not the most effective way to tackle piecing, because the scraps' varying grains tend to rub against each other, and the pieces often shift during stitching. The resulting quilt, while beautiful, tends to loosen and shred. This may be the reason there aren't many quilts of this style out there—they just didn't last long enough. The Maryland Kaleidoscope itself is so fragile that it is rarely put on exhibit anymore.

The Maryland Kaleidoscope takes its name from Lucy's 1913 note. Obviously, "Kaleidoscope" was what the family called the pattern. Unfortunately, Lucy does not say where the quilt pattern came from. We do know that in 1816 a Scottish clergyman-turned-scientist, Sir David Brewster (1781–1868), submitted a patent for a glass arrangement in a small metal tube: the kaleidoscope. Although he was granted a patent, something went wrong with the registration. By the 1830s, hundreds of thousands of kaleidoscopes had been manufactured and sold. They became a mania for people in every level of society, and their colorful, fractured interiors influenced styles on dishes, stained glass, and other expressions of decoration. Perhaps her cotton quilt's colorful piecing reminded Lucy Fitzhugh of her childhood toy and prompted the

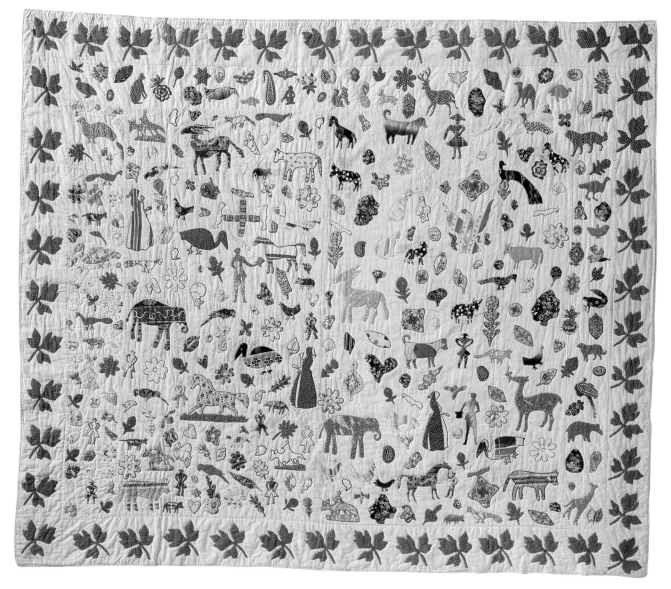

Figurative Appliqué | Date: ca. 1855 | Maker: Mary Ellen Crowbridge | Size: 78" x 65³/₄"

This may be another of those elusive quilts that bridge the cotton Kaleidoscope and Contained Crazies to the Victorian-era silk version. Surprisingly, it is signed on the back as from Wisconsin, which would have been a rough wilderness at the time. Many different motifs are cut from a variety of plain and printed cottons, then appliquéd to a muslin background in a style similar in execution to the Tiled Quilt. (See the Tile Quilt and "Stonewall" illustrations elsewhere in this book.) The figures are then outline embroidered to help them stand out. The wide variety of motifs include a kitten in a basket, an elephant, deer and elk, men on horseback, and a courting couple. Similar looks have been featured in British- and American-made appliqué quilts from this period, including one in Janet Rae's Quilts of the British Isles. (Collection of Robert and Ardis James. Photographs courtesy of the International Quilt Study Center.)

Dickens Cotton Crazy doll quilt | Date: ca. 1875 |
Maker: Unknown | Size: 14" x 14"

*The cheater print on the back of this rare doll quilt is based on Charles Dickens'
1836 novel,* The Pickwick Papers. *The madder browns and oranges in this print,
as well as the fabrics in the Crazy-pieced top, however, were popular in the 1870s,
not long after Dickens' death. (Collection of Mary Ghormley. Photographs by
Teressa Mahoney, Forever Yours Photography.)*

The Crazy was first mentioned in print in 1869, in the book *Our Acre and Its Harvest (A History of the Soldiers' Aid Society of Northern Ohio)* by Clark Brayton and Ellen F. Terry. The description is hardly complimentary:

> Above the grim surroundings of this busy corner hangs the "crazy bedquilt," a grotesque piece of newspaper patchwork, which is sold by lot every day, with the express condition that the unlucky possessor is not obliged to keep it, but will be allowed to present it to the fair. A considerable sum of money and a great deal of fun are realized by this transaction which takes place every noon just as the clock strikes twelve.

The speaker is Mary Brayton, who in February 1864 reported on a sanitary fair in Cleveland, Ohio, held to raise money for the Union cause. Sanitary fairs were similar to today's county fairs, and quilts in a wide variety of styles were often displayed there for fundraising purposes. It is clear that Crazy-style patchwork, while not desirable to the reporter, was also not unfamiliar to her.

Since newspapers, letters, and other papers were generally used only as a background foundation for cotton fabrics, it is probable that the quilt that Brayton ridiculed is yet another form of the cotton Crazy that earlier quilters pieced without a fabric foundation. Piecing on a paper foundation was not an unknown method for quilting, and the results were certainly more stable than a quilt pieced with no foundation at all. However, this quilt was pieced on cheap paper (newspaper) and considered a joke.

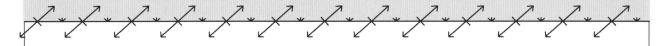

name. Or perhaps "Kaleidoscope" was a local or regional moniker. There are references to other Kaleidoscope quilts in inventory lists and family collections, but not enough information or description to help narrow the Maryland Kaleidoscope to any specific quilt style.

Other Early American Crazies

It would be easy to dismiss the Maryland Kaleidoscope as an aberration if it were the only one of its type in existence. The truth is, though, that at least a double handful of other Crazy quilts in this style have been discovered (although none outside the original thirteen colonies). Based on their fabrics and methods of construction, several Crazies fall within this narrow time period. Perhaps they were a minor trend based on the newly invented kaleidoscope.

One setting style is known as the Cross of St. Andrew. Its Crazy patchwork squares are separated by thick sashing, an arrangement generally known as a Contained Crazy. Several other examples exist in books and museum collections. All come from Pennsylvania and the New York Valley region, suggesting they were a trend there before 1850.

Although some of these early pieces use the same overall random pattern as the Maryland Kaleidoscope, a far more popular version was the Contained Crazy. For this style, randomly patched Crazy blocks are framed (or contained) with wide strips of prints or solids called sashing. Sometimes these Crazy blocks include smaller pieced blocks in their mix; sometimes they're mixed with other miniature-style pieced blocks in an overall sampler effect. So far at least, all of the early Crazies (or Kaleidoscopes) I know of from this time period originate from Pennsylvania, New York, or outlying areas. Were these early Crazies a trend there in the mid-nineteenth century? At least three quilts were known to have been made in the Ephrata-Lititz area of Lancaster County, Pennsylvania, about the same time, probably by Mennonite or Church of the Brethren members. (Interestingly, Crazies with Amish provenance, stitched much later, often using solid-colored wools or cottons, resemble this look much more than the quilts made by their Victorian non-Amish, or "English" counterparts.) Fabrics in these pieces vary; a wide variety of cotton prints, chintzes, and woven plaids and checks are used. (Perhaps the quiltmakers were using up scraps.) A number of the existing quilts, especially those with Mennonite or Brethren ties, mix in the bright orange, yellow, pink, red, and "blue-print calico gaiting" small-figured prints so beloved by Pennsylvania quiltmakers during that time period.

These early cotton Crazy-style quilts are remarkably similar:

- They contain a variety of cotton materials, including chintzes and calicos.
- Their fabrics may have been chosen in part for emotional connections to people and places.
- They're not elaborate, but simply pieced and simply quilted.
- They rarely contain much embroidery; if there's any, it's quite basic.
- They are often pieced as squares, strips, or other sections, then contained by sashing, or long strips of plain or print fabrics. The sashing helps minimize and stabilize any shifting or tension from the Crazy-patched squares.

Unlike their colonial forbears, which may have been created out of need, these Crazies seem to have been made for decorative purposes as much as use. But they hardly put on the fancy show that other quilt styles from the same period exhibit; quilt styles like Baltimore Album and broderie perse appliqué are much more elaborate and meant to be "best" quilts. It seems more likely that these Crazies were the workhorse quilts, meant to be used, but not prized.

Sometime before the Civil War, interest in the cotton-pieced Kaleidoscope-style quilt seems to have died down. Based on the comparatively few existing examples, it never was as popular as other patchwork styles from that period, like Irish Chain, Nine Patch, and elaborately appliquéd floral designs. We can easily come to that conclusion because the overwhelming majority of extant quilts from this period have few connections to the Crazy style. Considering the number of extant early nineteenth-century quilts out there in various patchwork designs (not that many, but some), and the relatively few early Crazy-style pieces in comparison, it is logical to assume that the early Crazy (or Kaleidoscope) was not made as often as its more traditional counterparts. Or it wasn't as popular a trend. Or it was too fragile to withstand the ravages of time as well as the other styles. Or a combination of these reasons. Quilt historian,

appraiser, and restorer Nancy Kirk believes that more early Crazies exist, but because they were generally not a "best" quilt style, they are locked away in chests or dusty attics and eventually will resurface as their caretakers pass away.

THE EMERGENCE OF THE CRAZY TREND

Sometime between the mid- and late nineteenth century, what we most quickly recognize today as a Crazy quilt, complete with embroidery and fancy fabrics, not only appeared, but became wildly popular. Sometime after the Kaleidoscope and early cotton Crazies, the Victorian-era Crazy, with its luxurious fabrics and lavish embroidery, was born.

It didn't appear out of nowhere. No quilt style ever does. Styles and patterns move in and out of popularity over the years, changing color and design as they go. Even the newest techniques and patterns have some basis, however small, in existing designs, styles, and work methods.

In spite of extensive research, no documentary evidence has been found to directly explain the jump between the workaday Kaleidoscope and the luxury-loving Crazy. But several key factors may well have influenced the Crazy style and fueled its explosion in the 1880s.

Handwork Was a Valued and Sought-After Skill

Fine needlework skills were not only taught in school, along with Latin and dancing, but they were also considered the marks of a lady. In her *Woman's Day Book of American Needlework*, Rose Wilder Lane observes, "[A] girl who didn't embroider was unheard of." In *American Quilts: The Smithsonian Treasury*, Doris Bowman mentions, "Until well into the nineteenth century, needlework was one of the few acceptable creative outlets for women."

Technique, however, was valued more than expression. Robert Bishop and Jacqueline Atkins, authors of *Folk Art in American Life*, note: "[W]omen's periodicals such as *Godey's Lady's Book*, *Miss Leslie's Magazine*, and *Peterson's Magazine* encouraged the use of pre-drawn patterns . . . [B]y the latter half of the nineteenth century, creative genius in this area was equated more with manual dexterity than with design."

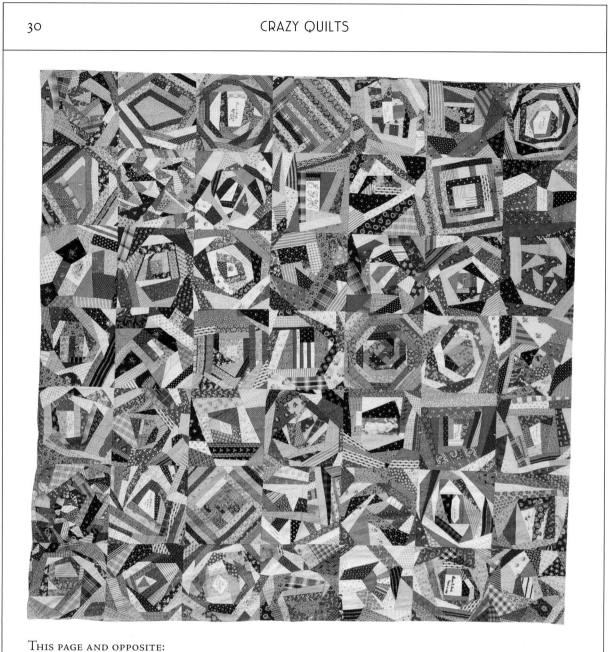

THIS PAGE AND OPPOSITE:

Double-Sided Crazy | Date: ca. 1889–1890 | Maker: Unknown group | Size: 78" x 78"

Several early Crazy-style quilts use the same construction as the Maryland Kaleidoscope. But this cotton Crazy signature top has a major difference—its blocks are pieced on a cotton foundation fabric. This quilt features primarily cottons with a few silk blends, and it is thought to have been made by the same women who signed it. (Rocky Mountain Quilt Museum. Photographs by Mellisa Karlin Mahoney, courtesy of Quilter's Newsletter.)

RIGHT: *This young woman is thought to be one of the contributors to the Double-Sided Crazy, which research suggests was made in or near Woolwich/Westport, Maine. Her plaid dress is very similar to scraps used on the Crazy-patched top side. (Rocky Mountain Quilt Museum)*

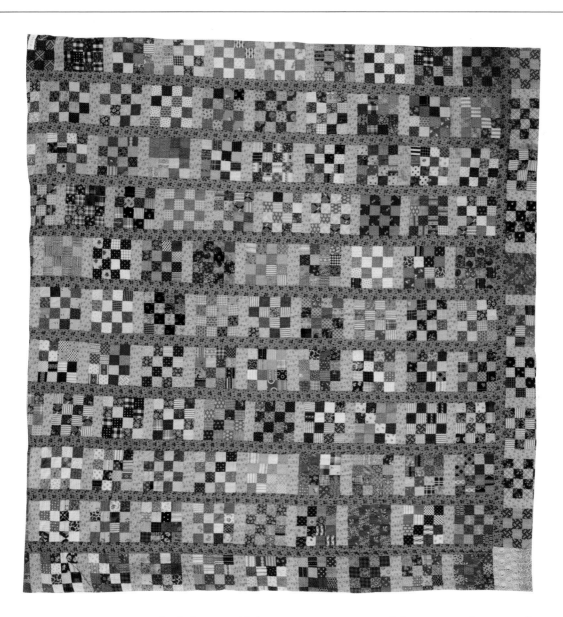

Many American periodicals began publishing in the thirty-year period before the Civil War, and their women's pages were filled with needlework patterns. Thanks to the availability of patterns, kits, and preworked items—both free and for sale—even those women with minimal sewing skills could have pretty things. Skill with the needle was valuable—and necessary—for keeping a household clothed, since the sewing machine was not commonly available until after the Civil War.

Silk Was Admired and Widely Used

The earliest pieced quilts are, almost without exception, pieced from cotton chintzes and prints. In the early nineteenth century, silk was a luxury item found mostly from the Orient, although smaller amounts were produced in France and other European countries. But by the end of the 1850s, thanks to increased trade with Japan, as well as strong ties with European silk manufacturers, silk had become "a feasible staple" to the American. As prices went down, silk gowns and wearables, as well as patchwork, became more common. In her 1859 *Ladies Hand Book of Fancy and Ornamental Work*, Florence Hartley praised the "rich mother who finds expensive silk, sewed in pretty patterns . . . for

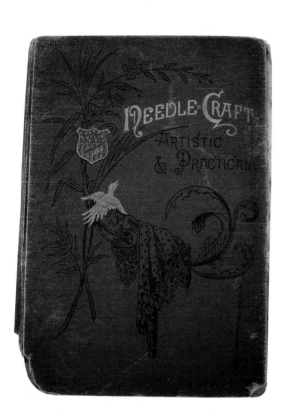

Books like Needle-Craft: Artistic and Practical, published in 1890, borrowed plentifully from magazines, and vice versa.

Luxury fabrics, especially silks, were favored for "best" clothing, fancy quilts, and home decorating in the nineteenth century.

her darling" and "the prettiest piece of work we almost ever saw": a star quilt pieced all of silks, with the lining of "pure white satin, from the skirt of mamma's wedding-dress."

Silk scraps could be put to good use with patchwork, as Hartley pointed out: "In an economical point of view there is great saving in patchwork quilts, if they are made from pieces of cloth already in the house, which are useless for anything else." If those pieces had a sentimental connection with festivities and happy memories, they were especially prized.

Floral designs, like this one pictured in the craft section of the September 1862 issue of Peterson's Magazine, *were popular for all sorts of needlework.*

This silk Chevron One-Patch Mosaic, made circa 1860, is unfinished; note the basting stitches still in place. Letters, printed pages, and old envelopes were cut into templates, then left in place while basting and stitching the fabric patches. (Collection of the author. Photographs by Teressa Mahoney, Forever Yours Photography.)

Other Foundation Techniques Were Growing in Popularity

Since colonial days, Americans had been exposed to English paper piecing, a technique in which fabric was basted over paper templates cut to the exact size of the pattern piece. The finished pieces were then whipstitched together in elaborate quilts. For those who used this technique, silk was just as effective a choice as cotton; basting silk pieces to a paper template kept them firmly anchored and held in place while the whipstitching was completed.

One specific English paper-piecing technique, pieced in ever-repeating hexagons, became the first American quilt pattern in print. Called the Mosaic pattern, it first appeared in Eliza Leslie's *American Girl's Book* in 1831, then in the January 1835 issue of the fledgling *Godey's Lady's Book*, where it was called "honeycomb-style patchwork." According to the magazine, "Each patch is joined to form a circle of five patches with one in the center." Although the magazine provided a wide variety of embroidery and other needlework projects, Virginia Gunn points out that the honeycomb or Mosaic was the only patchwork pattern given during *Godey's* first twenty years of publication. Eventually, magazines offered patterns for all kinds of template shapes, from

diamonds (for Baby and Tumbling Blocks quilts) to lozenges to even elongated hexagons. These were often recycled from past issues or "borrowed" from other publications (copyrights being loosely, if ever, enforced).

The first Mosaic quilts followed the medallion quilt style of their English and Continental forebears; the Mosaic pattern was part of a controlled central "medallion" area of a larger quilt, or it was used as part of the series of borders surrounding the medallion. Eventually, Americans preferred to use it as an overall pattern, often surrounded by a simple border. Although different template shapes could be combined, generally the same template was used repeatedly. This style was so ubiquitous that Florence Hartley referred to it just as "patchwork" in her book.

Letters, catalogs, and print advertisements were favorite sources for the hundreds, sometimes thousands, of scrap-paper templates needed for each quilt. Sometimes the paper was removed after the hexagon pieces were basted and whipstitched together, sometimes it was left in as a source of insulation. Early papers, which were made of linen or cotton, could not harm the fabric, but later paper, processed from trees and wood pulp, did.

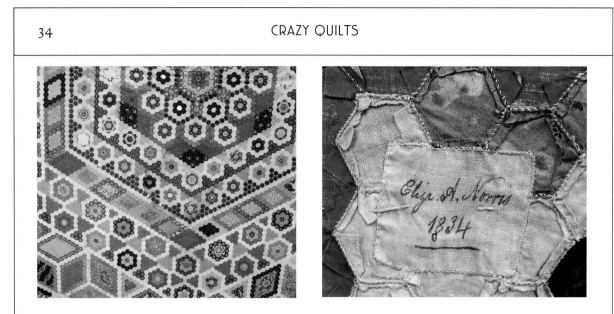

The English Medallion Mosaic quilt top pictured here is a precursor to the Grandmother's Flower Garden quilts so popular a century later. The backing signature panel reads "Eliza A. Norris 1834." If this top had been finished, we might never have known its maker. (Collection of the author. Photographs by Teressa Mahoney, Forever Yours Photography.)

All this care in positioning, cutting, basting, and whipstitching took time. An average Mosaic quilt—which was generally much larger-sized than today's pieces—could take several years to finish. By the Civil War, silk paper-pieced Mosaics, many with fabrics and embroidery similar to the later Crazy style, were extremely popular.

Although English paper piecing is probably quilting's oldest foundation technique, the best-known method today is the Log Cabin. The earliest signed and dated American Log Cabin is dated 1869, according to historian Barbara Brackman's quilt database. But the pattern appeared on sewing boxes as early as the mid-1700s and was even a woven pattern on Egyptian cat mummies. (Jane Hall, historian appraiser and Log Cabin historian, argues that its early origins are British, Manx, or even Roman.)

Early Log Cabin quilts were stitched, strip by overlapping strip, on a foundation of muslin, old or worn-out cotton clothing, or even feed or sugar sacks. (By the end of the century, paper, especially newspaper, was used as well.) Bonnie Leman and Judy Martin, authors of *Log Cabin Quilts*, note that because the Log Cabin could use up snips and strings of salvaged material too skimpy for other patterns, it was popular among pioneer women. Perhaps that is how

the pattern got its most popular name: it resembled the log homes of its earliest American makers.

Whatever its start, the Log Cabin quilt, pieced in silks, cottons, or wools, became a major fad in the last half of the nineteenth century. Log Cabin quilts were often used for fundraising or display at fairs during the Civil War. The foundation-piecing method allowed the quilter to not only stitch with "shifty" fabrics like silk, but also mix fabrics of different types and fibers, thanks to the stabilizing background fabric patches. Although its patches were generally evenly sized (widths could vary), its similarity to the Victorian Crazy quilt is too strong to be a coincidence. Virginia Gunn thinks so, too; in her book *America's Glorious Quilts*, she says, "[T]his type became very popular in the 1870s, although rural women often made them of wool or cotton instead of silk . . . they later adjusted this method to make crazy quilts." Cotton Kaleidoscope-style Crazy quilts continued to be made in the later nineteenth century, as well, but, like Log Cabins, were stitched on fabric foundations.

The popularity of the Log Cabin, later Kaleidoscope, and Crazy methods, with their foundation fabrics, argues that the average person at this time had more disposable income. Although foundation fabric could be cheap, coarse cloth or fabric too

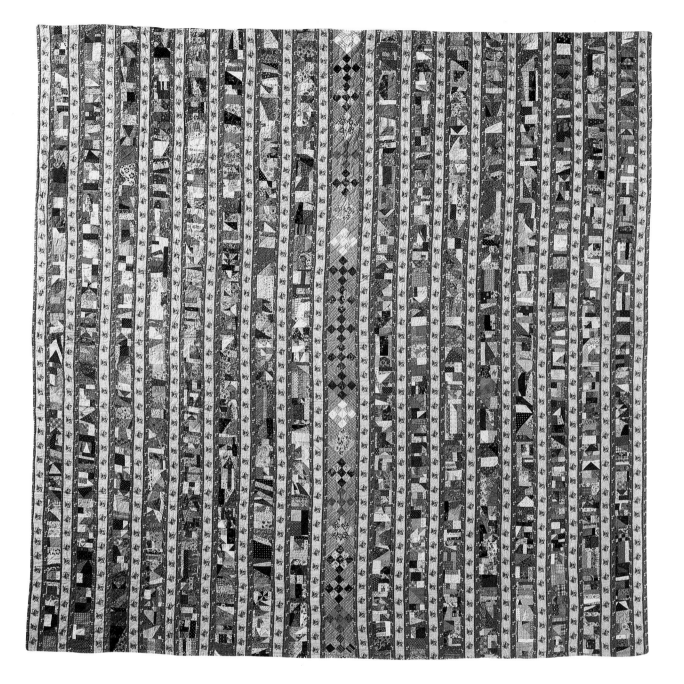

Strip Quilt with Nine Patch and Crazy elements | Date: ca. 1840 | Maker: Unknown | Size: 99 3/4" x 97 1/2"
Vertical sections of Crazy piecing alternate with Nine Patch blocks and printed strips in this very early Strippie-style quilt, pieced of cottons and linens. Very little is known about it, but its size, fabrics, and techniques suggest it was made about the same time as the Maryland Kaleidoscope. (Collection of Robert and Ardis James. Photograph courtesy of the International Quilt Study Center.)

badly damaged for other use, quilters still had to be able to afford to "waste" this extra fabric. Better-quality scrap pieces would be put to more visible use on the quilt top.

Probably the best-known Crazy from this time period is one in the Metropolitan Museum of Art's collection. That quilt's Crazy patchwork squares are connected by long sashing of a brown-stripe print, with no setting squares at the intersections. Its center inscription reads: "Made by/Mrs. Nancy Doughty/in the/82nd year of her age/for her friend/Miss Lizzie Cole. A.D. 1872." The fabrics are consistent with the date mentioned.

The Civil War Restricted Access to Fabrics and Ideas

The U.S. Civil War (1861–1865) had an inescapable effect on the quiltmaker's everyday lives. Magazines with patterns still were available during the war, especially in Union states on the East Coast, but mail service could not always cross easily over battle lines. Even if they could get the magazines, not many quilters could afford them when money became scarce.

Fabrics, thread, laces, and more were also hard to come by throughout both the South and the North. In their book *Southern Quilts*, Bets Ramsey and Merikay Waldvogel point out that "[s]eaports, once important conduits for imported British and French printed cottons and silks, were blockaded by the Union. Peddlers who formerly plied their wares along Southern byways did not venture out of Northern cities. Local cotton gins and textile mills, where Southern women sent their wool and cotton to be manufactured into thread, became military targets." Northern quilters had slightly better access to fabrics and notions, but Northern factories were focused on supplying fabric for soldiers' uniforms, not citizens' needs. The emphasis was on more practical fabrics like cotton, wool, and a mix of the two called linsey-woolsey. Every scrap was precious, and those too small for clothing could be used in quilts. It is no surprise that the Miniature Sampler, tiny blocks pieced and sashed together to form bed-sized quilts, became a

Traveling peddlers, like the one shown lugging his wares in this nineteenth-century illustration, were often a major source of fabrics and thread for rural quilters.

trend. (Many of these quilts have design ties to the Contained Crazy of a few decades previous.)

After the household sewing was done, the quilter could make a quilt from her dwindling scrap bag of luxury silks and fancy chintzes, the fabrics that represented happier times in the past. And in doing so, she could keep her mind busy and away from worry about her loved ones. Many "best" quilts from this period, silk and cotton alike, were intricately stitched, embroidered, appliquéd, quilted, and stuffed for a three-dimensional look. Such detail took more time, though no more fabric, to make, and a quilter could while away more months on just one piece. (Many of these same techniques reappear in the Victorian-era Crazy.) These elaborate quilts not only preserved women's sanity during the long uncertain days, but were sold during sanitary fairs and other fundraisers, as well. "Eager to do something for the cause, [women] had little to offer but their sons' and husbands' lives, their daughters' dowries, and their own domestic skills," says Barbara Brackman in *Quilts From the Civil War.* "Needlework, chief among their skills, became the war work that most occupied women in the Union and the Confederacy."

The End of the Civil War Brought New Influences and Materials

The end of the Civil War marked the beginning in a new era for America. Mail and goods of all kinds could easily crisscross the country thanks to the transcontinental railroad's completion in May 1869. Women's magazines, especially *Godey's Lady's Book*, wielded an influence on every aspect of domestic life, including needlework. In *Kansas Quilts & Quilters*, Barbara Brackman comments, "In the past, styles had changed slowly as women learned of new trends in face-to-face contact, one quilter at a time. The speed of change increased as national periodicals reached more farm families on the new rural free-delivery routes and as the technology for illustrations improved, allowing readers to exchange quilt patterns across the country." (Crazy quilts, according to Brackman, were one of the "first fads disseminated by ladies' periodicals.")

Manufacturers, their factories left quiet by the end of military contracts, were happy to begin producing fabrics and other textiles for the beauty-hungry public. *Labors of Love* authors Weissman and Lavitt note that by 1874, over $21 million worth of silks—including braids, ribbons, and embroidery thread—were being produced in America, a figure slightly under the amount being imported into the country at that time. By 1880, U.S. manufacturers were annually producing 800 million yards of cotton alone—at a time when the U.S. population was only approximately 60 million. Meanwhile, since the early 1800s, the "beginning of mass-produced printed textiles," European mills had been turning out tens of thousands of fabric patterns that used silks, wools, and cottons, and European imported fabrics were fervently copied by their American admirers. These new materials were priced attractively and contributed to the huge variety of fabrics, threads, and embellishments used in Victorian-era Crazy quilts.

Americans Were Fascinated by Oriental Designs

One of Crazy quilting's other names was *Japanese patchwork*—a name quite possibly inspired by the asymmetrical look favored in Japanese patterns.

Americans, as well as Europeans, had been fascinated with Oriental designs since colonial times. Early colonists collected Oriental-patterned *chinoserie* (dishware), imported from the East (mostly China) and copied by European pottery firms. By the time Japan loosened its trade restrictions in the 1850s, China had been trading for centuries, and customers were already familiar with the Orient's delicate porcelains, furniture, and silks. U.S. women's magazines had been publishing Oriental-themed embroidery designs since the 1830s; regardless of whether it showed a Japanese geisha in a kimono or a Chinese fisherman, all Asian designs tended to be pegged as "Chinese work."

After trade began with Japan, designers and other tastemakers sang the praises of Japanese art, and the new art of photography also promoted interest in the Far East. But the event said to truly ignite America's love affair with Oriental design—and serve as the primary inspiration for the Crazy style (according to some quilt historians)—was the 1876 Centennial Exhibition in Philadelphia.

World fairs were a new idea. In 1851, Great Britain held its "Great Exhibition of the Works of Industry," a lavish event conceived by Queen Victoria's consort, Prince Albert, and a British civil servant, Henry Cole. We know this event better by the name of the main building it was housed in: the Crystal Palace Exhibition. The exhibition was the first world's fair, and over the next fifty years, some forty international expositions were held all over the world.

The United States held its first such exhibition in Philadelphia in 1876. Because that year also marked the 100th anniversary of America's independence, the event was called the Centennial Exhibition of International Industry. (The official title was the International Exhibition of Arts, Manufactures and Products of the Soil and Mine.) At least thirty-seven (some sources say closer to fifty) countries were represented, including Austria,

Mikado Crazy | Date: ca. 1886 | Maker: Unknown | Size: 75" x 85"
This quilter tried to save money by using a less expensive "weighted" red silk for her border, which disintegrated. The backing fabric, shown in the detail image, was most likely inspired by Gilbert and Sullivan's Mikado. (Collection of the author. Photographs by Teressa Mahoney, Forever Yours Photography.)

"Madame Dragonfly" | Date: 2001 | Maker: Nancy Eha | Size: 57" x 56"
Nancy combined machine and hand piecing, appliqué, trapunto, silk ribbon embroidery, tatting, and folded fabric flowers in her "obsessively beaded" kimono-style Crazy. The name was influenced by Puccini's opera, Madame Butterfly. Note the photo transfer in the detail image; you'll see this J & P Coats "Katisha" trade card elsewhere in the book. (Photographs courtesy of the quiltmaker)

Mikado-themed trade card, ca. 1886. The fan position, according to the "flirtation" code, means "wait for me" or "come see me"—a message this beauty is also suggesting with her eyes!

Caucasian man in Oriental dress, ca. 1885. This man's queue (a long, pigtailed braid, unusual for a foreigner) and costume suggest he may have been a missionary or a performer.

Belgium, Brazil, Canada, France, Great Britain, Nicaragua, Portugal, Russia, Italy, Venezuela, China, and Japan. Officially opened on May 10, 1876, by President Ulysses S. Grant, the exhibition closed a little more than six months later, after nearly ten million visits had been logged. It was the first chance many Americans had to examine items (and people) from other cultures. And they were fascinated!

Japan may have seen the Centennial Exhibition as its chance to make an international impact. According to *The Illustrated History of the Centennial Exhibition*, $600,000 was appropriated for the Japanese exhibit. (In contrast, Great Britain, Australia, and Canada spent $250,000—combined—on theirs.) The Japanese exhibit was "filled in every part with a rich and valuable display, the variety and beauty of which were one of the great surprises of the Exhibition," one viewer noted.

In her book *Crazy Quilts*, Penny McMorris notes that the Japanese exhibit included several screens "of silk on light frames . . . painted and embroidered with scenes in the daily life of the people. The outlines of the figures and the landscapes were painted, and the costumes, faces, animals, and houses, etc., were worked out in relief with embroidery." (McMorris is actually quoting from *Frank Leslie's Illustrated Historical Register of the Centennial Exposition*, published in 1877.) One of these silk screens, with its "crazed," or patched, look, may have been the inspiration for the name "Crazy."

McMorris also points out that six years later, in 1882, *Harper's Bazar* credited the idea of a "mosaic patchwork of odd bits" they called "Japanese Patch" to an uneven pavement design shown under a priest's

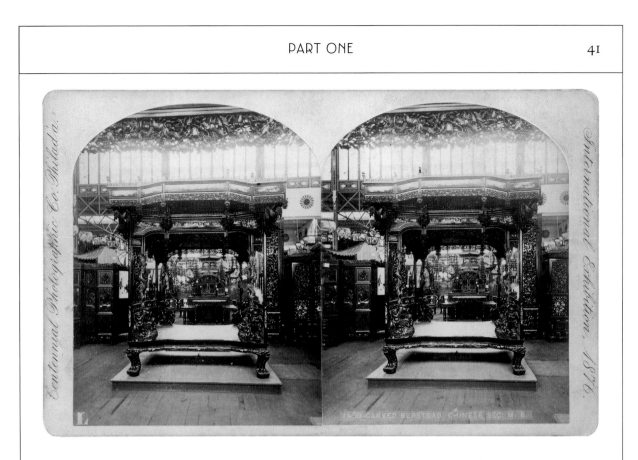

The Chinese Pavilion at the 1876 Centennial Exhibition in Philadelphia, Pennsylvania, is pictured in this stereoview. Notice the elaborate screens in the background.

feet in a panel of Japanese needlework. She asserts that "the primary source of this interest in Japanese design can be traced to direct contact with the Japanese art and artifacts shown at the Centennial Exposition and other later displays." But *Harper's Bazar* is unclear about when and where this Japanese panel was seen; the panel may or may not have been part of the Centennial Exhibition. Later, magazines picked up the design and expanded on it. A popular "cracked ice" design, found in magazines just before Crazy fever hit, may be related to this Japanese Patch look, as well.

On the other hand, Oriental patterns, textiles, and ceramics, including those of the Japanese, had already been influencing American and Continental design, including quilts. Randomly patched cotton quilts done in Crazy patchwork style existed well before the exhibition, as the Kaleidoscope quilts of colonial and pre–Civil War times show. Other so-called Japanese elements of Crazy patchwork were familiar to America and other countries long before

this, too:

- Embroidery had been practiced extensively on a variety of materials, and Oriental-themed embroidery designs had appeared in women's magazines since the 1830s.
- Painting had been used on everything from paper to porcelain to silk.
- Silk was not uncommon for use in quilts and furnishings.

Also arguing against the Japanese exhibit's ignition of the Crazy quilt trend are women's periodicals from 1876 and 1877, especially *Godey's Lady's Book* and *Peterson's Magazine*, the stalwarts of the Centennial Exhibition. Although the Japanese exhibit was a subject of great curiosity, the magazines' admiration is reserved primarily for the exhibits' porcelains and beautiful furniture instead of its needlework and textiles. Their praise is much more vocal for embroidery exhibits from Italy, Spain, Egypt, the Netherlands, Belgium, Sweden, and

Continued on page 45

There is no doubt that makers of the Victorian-era Crazy had a fondness for Japanese styles and motifs, especially at the time the Crazy trend reached full flower in the mid-1880s. Many a Crazy from this time period includes a kimono-clad geisha, a curved bridge, Japanese-style fans, and the quirky bugs and other flora and fauna that symbolized good luck and good fortune in Asian cultures. Was this Oriental influence from the 1876 Centennial Exhibition or something else entirely?

On March 14, 1885, a cheeky, playful new opera debuted in London to rave reviews. It went on to play for a record-breaking 672 performances and nearly two years straight. Within only a few months, it was being performed by musical companies touring America and Europe.

The new opera was William Gilbert and Arthur Sullivan's *The Mikado, Or the Town of Titipu*. Its story centers on Nanki-Poo, a "wandering ministrel, I, a thing of shreds and patches" who is really the son of the emperor of Japan, the Mikado. Nanki-Poo's efforts to woo his beloved, Yum-Yum, and foil his nemesis, Katisha, are complicated by the Lord High Executioner and his friend, Pooh-Bah. All sorts of mistaken identities and odd situations, highlighted by some of the funniest wordplays and songs in the Victorian period, occur before the young lovers are blessed by the Mikado and happiness ensues. Nanki-Poo's costume is often a patchwork-like mix of clothing, sometimes like Harlequin, his Italian predecessor.

Gilbert and Sullivan may have been inspired by a Japanese attraction in London in the 1880s: an elaborate living diorama depicting an authentic Japanese village. More than a hundred Japanese men, women, and children worked and played in five streets of Japanese-style houses set up in Knightsbridge. The faux village was created after Queen Victoria presented the Japanese emperor with a warship, and he had allowed some of his citizens to come to England to study the West; the village seems to have part of the emperor's gracious acknowledgment of the gift. The Victorians found this village fascinating. One onlooker said, "By their strange arts and devices and manner

A poster from 1885 advertises Gilbert and Sullivan's The Mikado.

of life, these chosen representatives of a remote race soon attracted all London. Society hastened to be Japanned, just as a few years ago Society had been aestheticized."

Gilbert visited the village with his wife, and later, in the *The Mikado*, he insisted on verisimilitude for his own Japanese village. The English performers wore costumes patterned after authentic costumes and made using Japanese fabrics. Gilbert even recruited a male

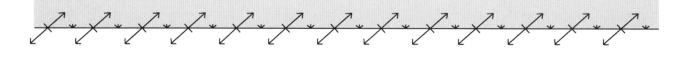

PISH-TUSH.

NANKI-POO.

A VIRTUOUS MAN,
LAND BEGAN,
HEREBY
TED.

COATS' THREAD

THE FLOWERS THAT BLOOM IN THE SPRING, TRA LA,
BREATHE PROMISE OF MERRY SUNSHINE,
AS WE MERRILY DANCE AND WE SING, TRA LA,
WE WELCOME THE HOPE THAT THEY BRING, TRA LA,
OF A SUMMER OF ROSES AND WINE,
AND SO, COATS' SPOOL COTTON IS ALWAYS A THING
AS WELCOME AS FLOWERS THAT BLOOM IN THE SPRING

KATISHA.

THERE IS MUSIC IN THE WHIRLING OF THE SPINDLE—
THERE IS MUSIC THAT THE CLICKING NEEDLE MAKES,
AND A SORT OF HAPPY FEELING
COMES GENTLY O'ER YOU STEALING,—
WHEN YOU USE COATS' THREAD THAT NEVER KINKS OR BREAKS.

J & P Coats brought out a series of Mikado character trade cards in the 1880s to advertise their thread. These feature Pish-Tush, a courtier and general toady (left); Nanki-Poo, the hero (center); and Katisha, the Emperor's "daughter-in-law elect" (right).

Japanese dancer and a geisha from the Knightsbridge village to coach the theater company. However, *The Mikado* was not as Japanese as it pretended to be. Many of the names were actually based on Chinese words and expressions; it makes references to "pigtails," or queues (single long braids for men), which only the Chinese wore at this time, and Japanese titles were sometimes changed.

But the inaccuracies didn't matter. People loved *The Mikado* so much that just the mention of its name became a potent selling tool. Soon advertising for merchandise of every kind—from calendars and toys to perfume and even thread—included Mikado characters. Japanese designs and goods of all kinds became the rage in America and Europe. There were "cheater cloth" prints designed to emulate Japanese-style patchwork and items featuring Japanese "embroidered" subjects; the latter were specifically labeled as "Mikado" prints. The kimono suddenly became a popular item of clothing, as well as a design element.

The Victorian-era Crazy was just reaching its greatest popularity when *The Mikado* became a hit in 1885. *The Mikado*'s influence on popular culture of that time is indisputable, and it seems more than possible that it could have had an effect on the Victorian-era Crazy.

Velvet Crazy | Date: ca. 1890 | Maker: Jennie Wallace | Size: 55" x 78¾"

Jennie used scraps and leftovers from her millinery business in Winnebago, Minnesota, to make this Crazy with herringbone trim.
(Minnesota Historical Society)

Continued from page 41
Russia. Exhibits of the Royal School of Needlework (in Britain) and Berlin-worked needlework (from Germany) were singled out for special attention.

Whether or not the Centennial Exhibition actually sparked the Crazy trend is debatable, but it definitely influenced the use of Oriental designs, luxury fabrics, and lavish embroidery techniques. Within a decade of the event, Victorian-era America would be in the throes of the Crazy craze.

THE RISE OF THE CRAZY TREND

A decade after the end of the Civil War, a new patchwork style began slowly rising in the thoughts of American quilters. In 1874, the editors of *Peterson's Magazine* featured an "ornamental fancy work" design using colored silk threads that seems to be a precursor to Victorian Crazywork. (It made use of the same fabrics and embellishments in the silk embroidered Mosaic, still popular in certain circles.) *The Country Gentleman*, in 1878, referred to an embroidered friendship canvas square as "a 'crazy' cushion, indeed"—a sign that Crazy patchwork was gaining recognition. And the November 1879 issue of *Peterson's Magazine* mentioned a "new work, which consists of scraps of all kinds being appliquéd onto serge, and ornamented with colored silks, in imitation of Eastern work. Stars, circles, and all sorts of shapes, are brought into use."

By 1882, more than one women's magazine had suggested sewing a Crazy quilt square by placing a plain square in the center of the block, then filling it in with other fabrics. (Similar patterns were unveiled in following years, some suggesting that strips be used to fill in the block, an effect that blurred the lines between the Log Cabin and the Crazy.) That same year, *Harper's Bazar* announced, "[W]e have quite discarded in our modern quilts the regular geometric design once so popular ... Now we are very daring. We go boldly on without any apparent design at all." And *The Farm and Fireside*, in its November 11, 1882, issue, published a long letter from a reader named Alice, who described "crazy or Japanese work" as "the most economical way to use silk pieces in patchwork." Alice said, "Any one who

has not seen work of this kind, has no idea how handsome it is, nor how fascinating to do."

Crazy Patchwork, a book published in 1884, promised to show "All the New Fancy Stitches Illustrated," and referred to "last year when crazy-work began to be talked of." According to the book, "The so-called Crazy-Quilt, which seemed destined to but an ephemeral popularity, has, within the last few months, gained a firmer hold upon the public mind; so that now the fancy for making such quilts is literally a craze."

By 1884, women's periodicals were flooded with information about the new trend. Reports emphasize the writers' surprise that Crazy quilting had taken hold, yet strongly suggest that the trend was happening long before they decided to report on it. (Interestingly, they never mention the cotton Kaleidoscopes or the cotton-pieced Crazies of only a few decades before.) Since *Godey's Lady's Book* and *Peterson's Magazine*, the top two women's periodicals, were both published in Philadelphia, their surprise at the silk Victorian Crazy style suggests that the trend did not begin in that cosmopolitan city. Could the switch from cotton to silk Crazies have begun in a rural area? The Olean Democrat, a newspaper in Olean, New York, published the following interview with a quilter on December 11, 1883:

> "Where did this idea of "crazy quilt" originate? Was the next question.
>
> "Well, I've been told all sorts of versions, but I believe that the truth is this: The officers' wives in a military post somewhere on the frontiers invented it. Of course it's only a new variation of an idea. Patchwork is as old as the hills. Silk patches are an innovation on the calico quilts of our grandmothers ..."
>
> Tell me why this particular style is called a "crazy quilt?" persisted the reporter.
>
> "O, for any number of reasons. Because the pattern is crooked, confused, confounded; because there's an infatuation in the work itself; because to see one is to want to make one; because in our search for pieces we drive dressmakers, milliners and dry goods clerks crazy."

Or the Crazy may have had a more unbalanced beginning, or so the catalog for Joseph Doyle & Co. (ca.1900–1915) insists:

> It may interest many to know that the first "crazy quilt" was made at Tewkesbury (Mass.) almshouse by a demented but gentle inmate, who delighted to sew together, in hap-hazard fashion, all the odd pieces given her. One day a lady visitor was shown the quilt as a sample of poor Martha's crazy work. The conglomeration of color, light and dark, of every conceivable shape and size, caught the visitor's fancy, and within a week she, herself, was making a crazy quilt. And thence the furor spread.

Whatever the origin of the term "Crazy quilt," it is helpful to remember that the one Victorian definition of "crazy" was "clever"—as in, "crazy like a fox!"

HEYDAY

Whatever its origins, by 1884, the year of its greatest fame, the Crazy had become king—the Victorian-style Crazy; that is, pieced primarily from silk scraps in velvets, satins, and all sorts of unusual weaves. (The wide variety of men's waistcoat and women's dress fabrics available, as well as customers' interest in the new and different, directly contributed to the Victorian Crazy's vivid look.) A multitude of embroidered and painted motifs decorated the patches; stitches and beads embellished their edges. The Crazy became an album of memories and beliefs, packaged by the needlework skills and creativity of its maker, and its fine fabrics testified to the wealth of the maker's family. "So ornate was much of this work that the primary function was no longer as a bedcover," writes Judith Reiter Weissman and Wendy Lavitt in *Labors of Love*. "[M]ostly, these pieces were made for show, and ended up in the parlor, where, thrown over a chair, they served to display their maker's talents for all to see."

The publications that somehow had missed the Crazy's appearance now hustled to make up for it by praising this new quilt style to the skies. "It is extremely doubtful whether this class of needlework will ever lose its popularity," gushed the Joseph Doyle & Co. catalog. "It serves so admirably to use odd bits of silk, and is really so artistic, if properly made, that its hold upon the feminine mind is never to be wondered at."

Artistic is a key word; Crazy patchwork rose to prominence at a time when art and design were being lauded and admired. John Ruskin, a theorist of style, posited that a happy society produced beautiful things—a thought that led directly to Aestheticism, the study of beauty for itself. Inspired in part by the 1876 Centennial Exhibition, as well as previous Oriental influences, this new movement advocated "art for art's sake." One of its strongest proponents was James McNeill Whistler, known best for his 1871 painting *Arrangement in Gray and Black: A Portrait of the Artist's Mother* (more often called "Whistler's Mother"). He said, "Art should be independent of all clap-trap—should stand alone, and appeal to the artistic sense of eye or ear. . . ."

Irish writer Oscar Wilde, author of the play *The Importance of Being Earnest* and the novella *The*

Continued on page 54

Oscar Wilde holds forth on Life and Art in this illustration from 1882. (Library of Congress)

The Crazy trend was a real boon to manufacturers, companies, and stores of the Gilded Age. So many different Crazy-quilt-related products and materials were offered for sale that it is impossible to list them all. First were the basics: sewing tools, threads, fabrics (bundles of scraps, containing enough fabric pieces to make a Crazy, generally sold for one dollar), laces, ribbons, and patterns. There were also matched sets of colored silk floss, books and instruction booklets, oil paints and patterns, stamping outfits that easily transferred designs for embroidery, or perforated patterns that helped position and trace the motif just so. Manufacturers also sold all of these items as part of "art needlework" embroidery kits.

For those whose needlework skills weren't quite up to par, there were commercially made appliqués, both hand- and machine-stitched. In appearance, these stitch-on appliqués were similar to today's iron-on appliqués, and some could be ironed in place, just like their modern counterparts. The resemblance, however, ends at price; the nineteenth-century embroidered appliqués were incredibly expensive. A sixteen-inch embroidered rose-spray pattern in the 1884 Ingall's catalog, for example, cost six dollars at a time when two dollars was considered a good daily wage. (These purchased appliqués are hard to notice in an antique quilt, unless you lean down and view the quilt at surface level. They stand up slightly from the surface, and the whipstitches used to hold them in place can be seen with closer examination. Such appliqués are much more common in antique Crazies than you would think!)

Some trade cards (small giveaway cards with pictures and patterns) even showed you how to stitch your own appliqué using your new sewing machine—if you were lucky enough to have a sewing machine. Thanks to the extensive stitch cards provided by sewing machine

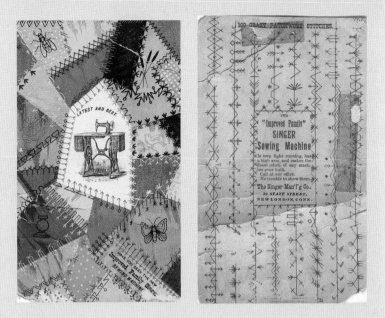

Promotional materials like this Singer Sewing Machine trade card—"100 Crazy Patchwork Stitches," circa 1890—encouraged quilters to use their machines to create fancy embroidery stitches, rather than stitching them by hand. The front and back of the trade card are shown here.

companies such as Singer, you could also do all sorts of embroidery work on the seams.

Entire hand-pieced and -embroidered Crazy squares were available for the handwork-challenged; purchase enough, and you could stitch them together for your own Crazy quilt. The Ladies Art Company's first catalog, appearing about 1895, offered such finished blocks, pieced in silk and embroidered in silk floss, for one dollar each. (Patterns and cotton-pieced squares cost considerably less.) Hand-painted squares and sections were offered for sale, as well. (These items were all made by women and children for starvation wages—the same people who were stitching fine shirts for pennies and hand-tinting pages in commercial magazines and books. (These poor working conditions were often discussed in the same magazines that benefited from them and that women read for patterns—especially *Godey's Lady's Book*—though these magazines were careful not to point out their own role in creating the conditions.)

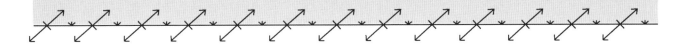

"My Crazy Dream" | Date: 1877–1912 | Maker: Mary M. Hernandred Ricard | Size: 74" x 68"

Mary stitched this outstanding quilt over nearly four decades, probably beginning with the embroidered schoolhouse center. A closer examination of the quilt reveals not only Mary's own Crazy patchwork, embroidery, and embellishments, but based on their staystitching and raised surfaces, a series of purchased floral embroidery details, as well. (International Quilt Study Center at the University of Nebraska–Lincoln, 1997.007.0541)

"Aesthetic Dress Crazy" | Date: ca. 1885 | Maker: Caroline Kountz Jones | Size: 72" x 65"

Caroline Kountz Jones was born in 1858 and made this quilt while living in Pittsburgh, Pennsylvania; otherwise, little is known about her. Caroline's quiltmaking skills, however, are undisputed. Silks, including velvets, combine with appliqué and embroidery. Undoubtedly, the Aesthetic movement heavily influenced Caroline's choice of motifs and contributed to the quilt's given name. (Los Angeles County Museum of Art)

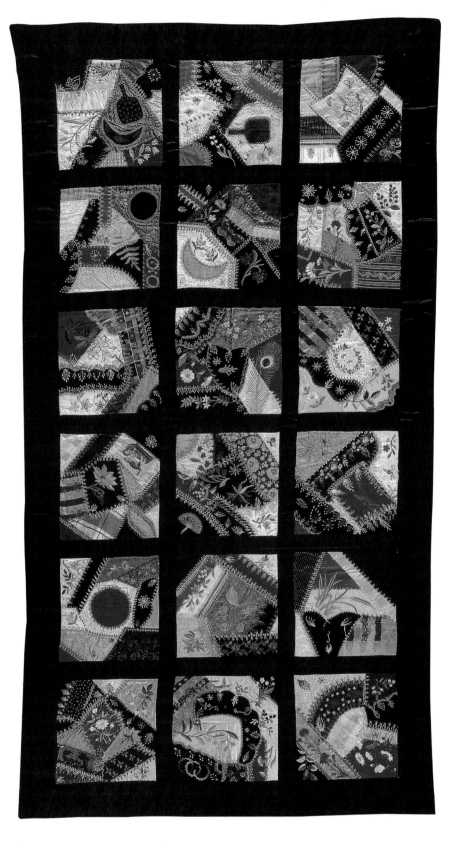

Crazy | Date: 1880 | Maker: Caroline Archibald | Size: 46¹⁄₂" x 86"

Aestheticist Oscar Wilde often wore a sunflower in the lapel of his favorite coat, which was dark purple lined with lavender satin. He loved lilies, often presenting armloads to people who pleased him. Lilies and sunflowers soon became symbols of the Aesthetic movement, along with peacock feathers, another Wilde favorite. All three motifs were stitched onto Victorian-era Crazy quilts; look for the peacock feather featured on this parlor throw. (Minnesota Historical Society)

The Crazy brought acquaintances to its Victorian-era festivities, including its predecessor, the now somewhat antiquated Mosaic quilt. Another was the Tile quilt, a form of Crazy or appliqué in which each shape or motif is separated by a thin border of fabric. According to Sue Fiondella, an appraiser and historian, New Yorkers knew the pattern as Stonewall, probably because it resembled the handmade rock walls that dotted the landscape of the northeastern United States. (At least one Crazy pattern done in similar fashion bears the same name.)

Probably the best-known relative to the Crazy, however, is the outline-embroidery quilt, known better as the Redwork quilt. The process of outlining various motifs, phrases, and designs with embroidery had been popular since the advent of a durable red dye for cotton, called Turkey red, in popular use by the 1830s. Invented by the Turks, this red dye used a multistep process, most of which we do not know today. Unlike nearly every other fabric and thread color available, Turkey red was colorfast, hard wearing, and remained bright after repeated washing and much use. A popular way to decorate household linens was to embroider their edges;

This larger-sized 4" x 7" "Holiday Greetings" trade card dates from circa 1875 and was given out compliments of Joseph H. Traeger in Bethlehem, Pennsylvania. Note the Tiled quilt on the little girl's bed.

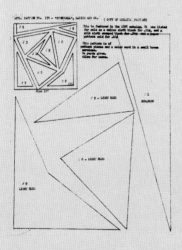

"Stonewall," an unusual quilt pattern, became the design bridge between Tile quilts and the Crazy. This Ladies Art Company rendition (No. 170) was mimeographed on thin cellophane in 1922, using pattern pieces first printed in 1898. Similar patterns are used today for a "stained glass" look. (Collection of Merikay Waldvogel)

since these linens were often boiled when being cleaned, Turkey red was nearly the only color that would remain intact. Eventually, redwork (Turkey red embroidery on a white background) became a design trend of its own and was a favorite method for teaching children how to sew. (It helped a lot of awkward adults, too.)

Outline stitch patterns were featured in periodicals and pattern books, and they could be purchased at the local dry goods store. Many of the same motifs appeared on Crazies, though usually in smaller scale and in different colors.

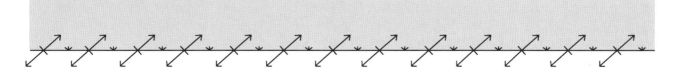

Garden Maze Redwork | Date: ca. 1900 | Maker: Probably a member of the Peacock family | Size: 82" x 95"
This unusual cotton twill and muslin Redwork quilt combines smaller blocks with a Garden Maze setting. Not only the blocks, but also the setting sashes are embroidered with a wide variety of images, including farm animals, Japanese maidens, teacups, water pitchers, and Sunbonnet girls. The quilt came from the Peacock family estate auction in Albany, New York. A number of quilts were sold, including some by Sylvia Peacock. If Sylvia made this one as well, we'll never know . . . "Think of Me" is embroidered in the center, but no name or initials. (Collection of the author. Photographs by Mellisa Karlin Mahoney.)

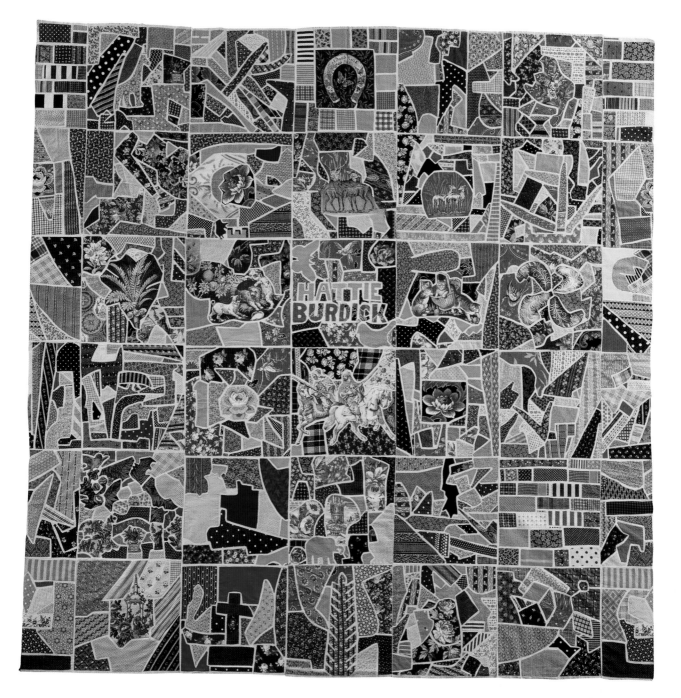

Tile Quilt | Date: ca. 1876 | Maker: Signed "Hattie Burdick" | Size: 81" x 80"

The Tile quilt style, so popular in the mid- to late nineteenth century, may have been one of those elusive links between the cotton Kaleidoscope and the silk Victorian Crazy. Each of the patches is "framed" with a thin edging of muslin in what we would call "Stained Glass" style today. Family tradition holds that this piece was actually made by multiple members of the Burdick family, rather than just the signer, Hattie Burdick. (International Quilt Study Center at the University of Nebraska–Lincoln, 1997.007.0163)

Continued from page 46
Picture of Dorian Gray, among many other works, was another Aesthetic proponent. Americans flocked to hear Wilde's conclusions on art and beauty during his 1882 lecture tour, which brought him not only to big cities like New York and Boston, but also to the mining camps and rough cities of the West. "Aestheticism," Wilde told them, "is a search after the signs of the beautiful. It is the science of the beautiful through which men seek the correlation of the arts. It is, to speak more exactly, the search after the secret of life." (By lecture's end, the secret of life would be suddenly revealed: art.)

Cultural societies sprang up, inspired in great part by Britain's Royal School of Art Needlework. One magazine, *The Art Amateur*, wrote, "It is the fashion to talk about art and, in a fashionable way, to practice it. Young ladies, instead of spending their mornings at the piano . . . take lessons in painting on china, in oils, or water-colors, or ply their nimble fingers in the production of 'art needle work.'" (Sometimes those groups, like the ones formed by Candace Wheeler in New York City and Queen Victoria in Kensington, generated income for young gentlewomen impoverished by the century's wars and financial unrest.)

The Aesthetic movement was in full bloom during the heyday of the Victorian Crazy. The growth of the "Art is Beauty" movement contributed to the rise of the Crazy by encouraging a woman to use her talents and materials in a visual, pleasing manner—especially when it came to the family home. Home and family were considered a woman's primary calling, and she was expected to make the home a cozy and welcome environment, regardless of her income. By the time Crazy patchwork came to the fore, she was already surrounded by the trappings of various decorative movements, most of which used rich, textural materials, lavish embroidery, laces and other handwork, and a variety of interesting surfaces. Virginia Gunn says, "By promoting new types of embroidered bed coverings and rejecting calico patchwork as artistic needlework . . . women wishing to participate in the art movement and to continue making quilts required new forms of expression. Crazy quilts and outline quilts emerged as grassroots responses to Aesthetic Movement fashions."

Designers such as Christopher Dresser were influential in using Orient-inspired design for not only ceramics, but also furnishings. Their work soon became a booming trend in European and American households. The aesthetes greatly admired Japanese design and decorated with fans, umbrellas, and the birds and insects that represented good luck and wisdom in Oriental culture; owls, also signifying wisdom, were special favorites. These symbols often made their way into the Crazies of the period.

Although only middle or wealthy classes were able to fully indulge in the Aesthetic credo of beauty for its own sake, even the poorest servant liked to think of herself as someone with possibilities. Her family needed a comfortable place, as well, and what better way to make it so than with her own delicate handwork? It would be just another proof that she, like her "betters," was just as much a lady as they were—even if she did have to work.

POPULAR CRAZY THEMES

Crazy quilts are filled with ideas in picture form. Sometimes the pictures are crude outlined representations; sometimes they are sophisticated, satin-stitched, three-dimensional portrayals. Ribbons, cigarette or tobacco silks, old clothing and other fabric leftovers, painted panels, even photos—all these materials made their way into Crazies, in addition to fabric scraps. And all were used to portray a wide variety of motifs and themes.

Advertisements

When the Crazy quilt movement hit, manufacturers were quick to jump on board. For the first time, the country was linked by railroad (see "Transportation"), and everything from sewing machines to quilting fabrics could be easily shipped from coast to coast. Leftover pieces of silk or cotton, even bits of thread and trims that were formerly thrown away, could now be marketed as scrap bags. Several companies marketed embroidery catalogs and stamping outfits (kits with patterns, dyes, and tools for tracing) in magazines

ABOVE AND BELOW: *Trade cards were given out free by a wide variety of companies, and they were avidly collected in scrapbooks and photo albums well into the twentieth century. These three cards promote machine embroidery via the Davis Vertical Feed Sewing Machine ("pioneers and leaders in sewing machine decorative art work"); Ivars & Pond pianos; and even hair remover! Cherubs, a popular subject for Crazy quilts and Redwork, were thought to represent children, living or dead, or to act as their guardian angels.*

such as *Harper's Bazar, Peterson's Magazine, Godey's Lady's Book,* and *McCall's.*

What these enterprising companies did not realize was that quilters could be even more resourceful than they were. Artwork from the companies' ads and trade cards became popular motifs on Crazy and Redwork quilts. Quilters often copied ads that included flowers or figures of ladies and children. One of the most popular ads copied was a Cuticura brand soap ad featuring a baby curled up in a soap dish.

Animals, Bugs, and Other Creatures

Farm animals, including horses and chickens, were often stitched on Crazy quilts. People of the Victorian era often kept a horse for transportation and a small pen of chickens or a cow for food. Cows were a bit rarer in the Crazy, though they were often pictured on the Crazy's sister trend, the Redwork quilt.

Owls, a favorite of the Aesthetic movement, stand for wisdom, and often appear on Crazies wearing spectacles and/or with quirky sayings embroidered underneath.

The most popular creatures on Crazies, though, are dogs and cats. These appeared in both realistic and comic form and were often accompanied by children. Sometimes the animals are dressed as if they were children!

Bugs have a surprising place on Victorian-era quilts. Crickets, flies, and even cockroaches were Oriental symbols of good luck and good fortune, and were embroidered on Crazies and Redwork quilts. Other insects, like the bee, represented hard work and industry.

The Crazy's favorite creature symbol, however, is the spider web, another Far Eastern symbol of prosperity. Although folklore says a spider and/or spider webs should be worked into every Crazy, usually in embroidery, they are not as common as thought.

Children

Children were some of the Victorian age's greatest joys, but also its sorrows. Children in the nineteenth century were subject to cholera, typhoid, smallpox, measles, mumps, and other diseases that today are preventable. Other childhood dangers were directly connected to poor sanitary conditions, especially in the cities. In 1870 Chicago, for example, where the sewage-filled Chicago River flooded into low-lying areas after rainfalls, children had a fifty-fifty chance of dying before age five. The odds were even lower for children age two and under. (By 1900, civic and medical improvements had raised the odds to 75 percent—not as good as today's 98-plus percent, but better.) At least one of every four children died. (Miscarriages only increased this figure.)

It was not uncommon to wait days, weeks, or even months before naming babies, to see first if they would survive. Pincushions with "Welcome, Little Stranger" spelled out in pins were a popular new-baby gift. Children's lives were so easily snuffed out that often their first photo was taken post-mortem, as they were held in a grieving parent's arms.

Children who managed to survive were very precious to their parents. If those parents were wealthy, life was fairly easy; if they were poor, then children began working at a very young age. Sometimes they worked alongside their parents at home; sometimes they sold items on the street, or became servants in the homes of those better off. The Industrial Revolution had begun, and many children went to work in factories.

In spite of the grimy reality, it was much nicer to think of childhood as unending pleasure, and children's book illustrations of the time generally promoted this concept. In the forefront of children's book illustration was Kate Greenaway, a British artist whose idealized drawings of children became the epitome of graceful elegance. She called the children she drew *mignonettes,* or "little sweeties," and dressed them in the Regency-era fashions that had been popular decades earlier. The wealthy public was so taken with her little girls in high-waisted Empire dresses and bonnets, and little boys in gentlemanly "Little Lord Fauntleroy" suits, that they began dressing their children that way. Greenaway's illustrations were admired and openly pirated around the world, but especially in America. Greenaway-style items,

Redwork Crazy | Date: 1885 | Maker: Signed R. R. Mains | Size: 80" x 85"
Yes, Crazy and Redwork quilts were made during the same time period—this piece is proof of it! Nothing is known of its origins, but this unusual piece's date marks it as made during the height of interest in the traditional Victorian silk Crazy. The maker Crazy-pieced various muslin patches on a fabric foundation, then embroidered over the seams and added a variety of barnyard-themed motifs. (Collection of Toni Baumgard. Photographs by Mellisa Karlin Mahoney.)

Crazy | Date: ca. 1910–1920 | Maker: Possibly mother of Georgia Rounds (born 1914) | Size: 67" x 59"

Owls were a traditional symbol of wisdom—and a favorite of Victorian-era quiltmakers. This quilt also contains embroidered handkerchiefs, painted velvet, and a variety of ribbons ranging from the G.A.R. to a sofa care tag! (Minnesota Historical Society)

Little Red Riding Hood finds "Granny" snuggled under a cotton Crazy coverlet in this 1920s advertising booklet.

including postcards, wallpaper, dolls, and plates, were everywhere.

Greenaway's pictures of children, both her originals and those of imitators, are stitched on many Crazy quilts, usually in line or satin embroidery. Their presence is not only a reminder of a famous illustrator, but also of the quiltmaker's cherished children.

Flowers

Crazy quilts are filled with flowers! Flowers are shown meandering down vines, spilling out of cornucopias, or collected in tussie-mussie (posy) holders. Quiltmakers painted and embroidered flowers on their quilts, as well as using fabrics or trims that had floral designs. Regardless of how a maker incorporated flowers into her work, growing evidence suggests that her choice of flowers was anything but random.

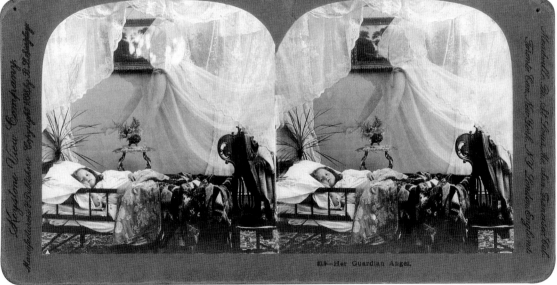

"Her Guardian Angel," 1898 Keystone stereoview. Angel caretakers, even shadowy ones, were a great comfort to anxious mothers during this period of high child mortality.

Crazy Quilt Teddy Bears | Dates: 1993 (small bear), 1995 (large bear) | Maker: Cindy Notarianni Swainson | Sizes: 9" x 13" and 11" x 16"

Cindy Notarianni Swainson Crazy-pieced the smaller bear in Southwest-inspired colors and motifs for her sister Lissa. After Lissa's death, her will deeded the bear back to the quiltmaker. The larger bear is filled with embroidered memories of the Swainson family's life in Toronto, Canada, and Colorado, including native wildflowers from both Canada and the American West. (If you look closely, you can see the columbine, Colorado's state flower, as well as daisies and trillium.) Both bears are fully jointed; the larger one took more than 140 hours to construct. (Collection of the quilt-maker. Photographs by Mellisa Karlin Mahoney.)

These postcards, printed circa 1915 to 1920, use meanings from the Language of Flowers and include a popular series featuring a flower (or grain) on each card. Each month of the year traditionally has a birthstone assigned to it, as well as a flower. Note the birthday postcard at top left: It combines the April tulip with the emerald, usually assigned to May. (Someone at the card company must have goofed!)

For hundreds of years, a theory called the Language of Flowers assigned a specific meaning to every green and growing thing. It seems to have stemmed from two sources. One was the Western European use of floral symbolism, plus flower meanings from religion and herbal medicine, for everything from mythology to heraldic symbols. The second source was the Turkish *selam*, or language of objects, by which coded messages could be sent using certain symbolic objects. As Lady Mary Wortley Montagu, whose husband was the English ambassador to Constantinople from 1716 to 1718, explained to a friend, "There is no color, no flower, no weed, no fruit, herb, pebble, or feather that has not a verse belong to it; and you may quarrel, reproach, or send letters of passion, friendship, or even news, without ever inking your fingers."

The first English flower language book, *Flora Domestica, or The Portable Flowers*, was published by Elizabeth Kent in 1823. One of the most popular American volumes was *Flora's Interpreter; or, The American Book of Flowers and Sentiments* by longtime *Godey's Lady's Book* editor Sara Josepha Hale, first printed in 1830. It provided meanings not only for flowers, but also for fruit, herbs, and trees.

Genteel young Victorian ladies were required to learn the rudiments of the Language of Flowers along with their usual lessons in deportment, dancing, needlework, and French. Catherine Waterman, author of a book on the subject, wrote in 1839, "The Language of Flowers has recently attracted so much attention that an acquaintance with it seems to be deemed, if not an essential part of a polite education, at least a graceful and elegant accomplishment."

The rose was a great favorite with the Victorians. According to the Language of Flowers, different types and colors of roses had the following meanings.

* **Rosebud:** a confession of love; untried love

* **Rose in full bloom, combined with two buds:** "you are beautiful"

* **Red:** true love (deep red also meant bashfulness)

* **Black:** a harbinger of death

* **White:** girlhood, naiveté, purity

* **Peach:** modesty

* **Pink:** motherhood

* **Yellow:** jealousy, infidelity

Roses, like the ones shown on these 1920s post-cards, represented the highest form of love.

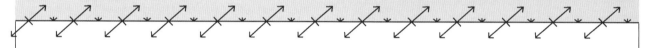

Many a romantic maiden studied her dictionary on the Language of Flowers to try and decipher the meaning behind the bouquet she'd just received from an admirer. She might also consult it in order to know what kind of nosegay to send her rival as a warning; a nice bouquet of peonies (indicating anger and/or ostentatiousness), lavender (distrust), and pennyroyal ("run away as fast as you can!") would do the trick.

Popular floral motifs on Crazies include pansies ("you occupy my thoughts; think of me"), violets (faithfulness), carnations (pure and deep love, or, if the carnations are red, "Alas for my poor heart!"), cornflowers (delicacy), forget-me-nots ("remember me"), lilies (purity, modesty), lily of the valley (return of happiness), and water lilies (eloquence, purity of heart). Daisies were a favorite of quilters, perhaps for their meaning (beauty, innocence), but also perhaps because they were easy to embroider and paint!

The Language of Flowers was very important to Victorian-era quilters. Though Crazies of the time are full of flowers, quilters were very, very careful not to use those with negative meanings. After viewing literally thousands of flower-covered Crazies, I've noticed an astonishing lack of the "bad" flowers. The rare exceptions are those quilts whose maker may deliberately have tried to hurt the recipient. Certified appraiser Vivien Sayre saw one such Crazy brought in for a documentation day at the New England Quilt Museum. It included black roses (which meant sickness and death), plague rats, and embroidered daggers dripping blood. According to the owners, the quilt had been made for a man and his new wife by the woman he had jilted some time before.

Hobbies and Pastimes

The first bicycle was invented about 1790. Its second version, in 1816, had wheels but no footpedals—it was meant to be pushed, scooter style. As bicycling gained popularity with the average public, bicycle races were held, couples flirted on bicycles built for two, and bicycling joined the long list of amusements to be pictured on Crazy quilts. Other pictured pastimes included

Crazy | Date: ca. 1880–1900 | Maker: Unknown | Size: 53" x 52"

A central panel of silk ribbon and chenille-worked roses gives this quilt a gracious quality. It may have been made in Indiana; the maker remains unknown, in spite of the initials "I. H." Note the many floral details, as well as the patriotic eagle block at bottom left labeled "14th M. C.," probably the U.S. Marine Corps. (International Quilt Study Center at the University of Nebraska–Lincoln, 1997.007.0284)

A young man celebrates his collegiate ties in this unusual 1880s photo. Note the Harvard-themed silk on the Crazy pillow in the chair.

horse racing; tennis, squash, and other racket sports; baseball; football; rowing; and much more. Motifs from these sports were also depicted in cotton shirting prints, which eventually becoming known as "conversation fabrics." The latter sports were also printed on silks. Both types of fabric appeared in Crazies, though cotton prints were used most often, especially in the popular all-cotton Crazies of the 1890s. Sometimes sport motifs with college insignias or images of college sports teams were printed on cigarette and tobacco silks.

Love and Longing

Romance has been a universal emotion ever since man turned to woman, and Victorian Crazies celebrate it. In fact, many a Crazy seems to have been made to celebrate a wedding. Initials, dates, and figures of couples have all been stitched or painted onto Victorian Crazy quilts; cigarette silks with images of couples were sewn into Crazies, too. One popular motif was linked rings; these may represent weddings, although they may also have been Masonic or Odd Fellows symbols, number

representations (indicating the number of a members or children in a family), or even commemorations of the Olympic Games.

Fans, a common feature in Crazy quilts, were not only a good luck symbol from the Orient, but also a popular decorating accessory in the Victorian household. Even the most modest budget could accommodate a pretty paper fan for display on the wall or mantelpiece. Fans were also a popular and practical ladies' fashion accessory. Unspoken society rules dictated that men and women should not speak freely to each other, so women would communicate—and flirt—with men by using their fans instead. These "flirtations" were studied as avidly as the Language of Flowers for secret hints and meanings.

It is rare to find a Crazy quilt without a fan, either fully or partly open. Most often, fully opened fans (meaning "wait for me" or "I'm interested") are displayed in one or all four corners of the quilt.

Mourning and Memories

Death was a near and constant presence for Victorian-era Americans. Disease, poor sanitation conditions, and accidents were common. Women and children frequently died during childbirth, or afterward were too weak to survive infections. And of course there were wars to be endured during the Victorian age, beginning with the U.S. Civil War and moving into World Wars I and II.

The Civil War was of special significance to Victorian Crazy quilters; most women had lost at least one relative, if not more, in the conflict. Returning Union soldiers formed the Grand Army of the Republic (G.A.R.) in 1866. The United Confederate Veterans (U.C.V.) was not formed until 1889. (Both groups have descendant organizations today.) G.A.R. ribbons especially were frequently incorporated into Crazy quilts, although Confederate-themed ribbons occasionally appeared, too.

Victorian women who lost loved ones, regardless of the reason, were expected to go into mourning for two to three years; the first twelve to eighteen months were spent in "deep mourning," and the rest of the period was "full" or "half mourning." They were expected to wear black during the entire period, unless the

Cigarette Silk Quilt | Date: 1912 | Maker: Unknown | Size: 54" x 66"

University-themed cigarette silks make up the majority of this interesting piece—with flags thrown in, as well! The quilt is marked "LA, California: 1912." (Collection of Maury Bynum. Photograph by Melissa Karlin Mahoney.)

widow was young—then lavender or light gray could be substituted. Men wore black suits or armbands, and their period of mourning was much shorter. Wearing black was more difficult than it seemed; until the 1880s and the advent of artificial fabric dyes, black fabric dyes were frequently unstable. Black clothing would fade, or it would bleed dye, ruining underclothing and staining the skin.

Since photos and other mementos were few, the deceased's clothing was preserved and could be used in a memorial quilt. One suspects that many a quilt, Crazies included, utilize this kind of fabric, though it is not always evident. "Quilts made from the clothing of loved ones were and still are among those most cherished, and are frequently passed down in a family because of their sentimental value," Reissman and Lavitt point out in *Labors of Love*.

Even hair was embroidered into Crazy quilt seams! This is not surprising, given that hair from dead loved ones, old and young, was often displayed in lockets and pins, woven into bracelets and watch fobs, or arranged in a "hair wreath" for wall display. In the case of children, hair and clothing may have been the only remnants of a young life to their grieving parents. Adding initials and names of dead loved ones to a quilt also preserved the quiltmaker's past connection with them.

Britain's Queen Victoria was perhaps her age's chief mourner. She entered widowhood with her consort Albert's death in 1861 and never really left it for the next forty years. The "Widow of Windsor" dressed in mourning for many years; her subjects followed her lead and used rich, darkly shaded, jewel-toned materials not only in clothing, but also for home decorating. The Americans quickly followed suit, using burgundy, black, forest green, brown, and other dark-toned fabrics for their homes and dress. These colors and fabrics were popular ingredients in Victorian-era Crazies.

When an important American figure (usually a president or governor) died, citizens wore mourning ribbons often printed with the deceased's image, pertinent dates, and sometimes popular quotes. Mourning ribbons were first worn after the death of George Washington and have reappeared for every deceased president since then, including Ronald Reagan and Gerald Ford. These ribbons were often added later into quilts, cushions, or display pieces as a sign of respect.

Occupations and Organizations

A fond quilter would include not only her husband's initials (and possibly his clothing) in her quilt, but items that pointed to his work, political affiliations, former military status, and favorite groups, as well. A farmer's wife might paint or embroider pictures of farm animals onto her quilt, for example, or use a related motif. For example, Poppies (remembrance) were used to signal a wartime experience. (Eventually they became a symbol of the American

THIS PAGE AND OPPOSITE: *Members of fraternal organizations like the Masons and Woodmen of the World, as well as Civil War veterans, were proud to show their connections by wearing ribbons. These were carefully saved and used as bookmarks, then stitched into quilts or other decorative items.*

By the end of the nineteenth century, it was not uncommon to find pocket-size, nicely printed "flirtations" books included along with Language of Flowers glossaries. Most probably were meant to be given as gifts. One 1871 booklet called *Little Flirt* has gold-edged pages and fine printing, yet fits in the palm of the hand. Here are its instructions for communicating by fan:

* Drawing the fan across the face and/or lips: "I wish to speak to you."
* Carrying the fan in the right hand: "You are too willing."
* Holding it in front of the face with the right hand: "Follow me."
* Carrying it in the left hand: "I want to make your acquaintance."
* "Accidentally" dropping a fan (a favorite ploy in old movies): "We will be friends."
* Fanning yourself quickly: "I am engaged."
* Fanning slowly: "I am married."
* Opening and shutting the fan quickly: "You are cruel."
* Holding the fan open wide: "Wait for me."
* Holding the fan closed: "I have changed."
* Holding the fan with handle to the lips: "Kiss me."

A woman poses for the camera with fan in hand.

Gift books, like this Little Flirt *(1871), were popular presents from admirers, but "Flirtations," like the Language of Flowers, were often listed in encyclopedias and household help books, too.*

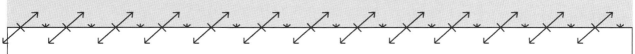

legion.) Or she might choose her husband's favorite tool or organization motif. (Masonic symbols are some of the most popular insignias used.)

The stars of many Crazy quilts, though, were printed ribbons, usually silk, from trade organizations and conferences given out both for special and commemorative events, and also used to signify membership. These widely varied in size and color, especially the souvenir ribbons, but were proudly worn by those who were participating. If she believed in the same cause, the clever quiltmaker snagged the ribbon her husband brought home from his latest meeting and put it to good use in her Crazy quilt.

Victorian Fan Crazy | Date: ca. 1885 | Maker:
Unknown | Size: 53" x 60"

*Fans are a prominent part of Victorian Crazy quilts, and this one
has its share, along with fancy stitching and floral motifs. A black
velvet border richly contains the pieced top. (Collection of Maury
Bynum. Photographs by Mellisa Karlin Mahoney.)*

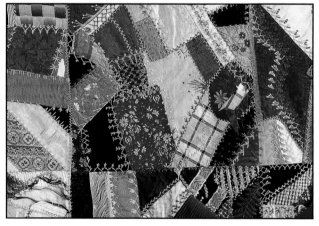

G.A.R. Crazy quilt top | Date: ca. 1890 | Maker:
Unknown, probably Ohio or Iowa | Size: 70" x 80"
Many of the ribbons in this silk Crazy commemorate "encampment"
celebrations of the Grand Army of the Republic, a Civil War
Northern veterans' organization. (Collection of the author.
Photographs by Teressa Mahoney, Forever Yours Photography.)

Ribbon pillow top | Date: ca. 1890 | Maker: Unknown, East Coast | Size: 30" x 30"
Silk ribbons like these were brought home as treasured souvenirs of special events and gatherings. Note the scarce (and valuable) 1885 President Ulysses Grant mourning ribbon. (Collection of the author. Photograph by Teressa Mahoney, Forever Yours Photography.)

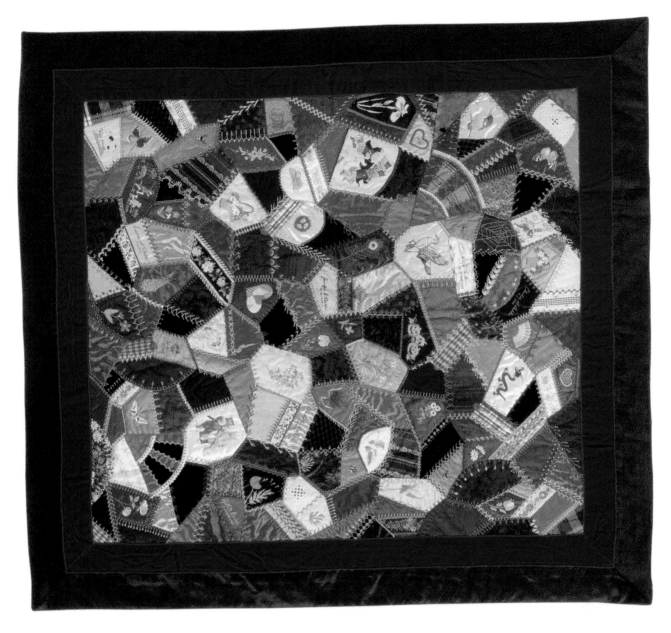

Family Signature Crazy | Date: 1995 | Maker: Christine Dabbs | Size: 47" x 52"

Signatures of family members, some who have since died, cover this memory piece. It is entirely hand-stitched, using silks, satins, brocades, and ribbons. The seams are covered in cotton and silk thread, then accented with beads. Many of the embellishments have a personal meaning; the duck outline is a copy of a 1950s pen-and-ink drawing by Chris's father, for example. This piece won first place in California's Marin Quilt and Needle Art Show in 1995 and was exhibited at Quilt Expo V in Lyon, France, the next year. (Collection of the quiltmaker. Photographs by Mellisa Karlin Mahoney.)

People

If someone was important to a quiltmaker, his or her face, name, or initial could easily end up on her Crazy quilt. Also popular were signature Crazy quilts, pieced from patches of fabric sent to famous figures to sign in ink. (Sometimes the signatures were embroidered over later.) Signatures from politicians and historical figures were the overwhelming favorites.

Crazy quilts have included pictures of everyone from John L. Sullivan (a famous boxer) to not-so-respected actresses pictured on cigarette silks. Cyanotype photos printed on cotton cloth—which have the look of blueprints—were a way for people to include their own photos in their quilts. Sometimes photos were printed on the fabric in black and white shading, then hand-tinted.

Redwork and other outline stitching was another way to add familiar faces to quilts. The "Pan Am" Redwork quilts are particularly wistful in this respect. Collections of redwork-embroidery patterns were sold at the 1901–1902 Pan American Exposition in Buffalo, New York. Some patterns depicted the solemn features of President William McKinley, who had been shot while visiting the Pan Am's Temple of Music, and the words "Our Martyred President." McKinley's vice-president and successor, Theodore Roosevelt, and both men's wives, were also included on some Pan Am patterns.

Politics and Patriotism

Politicians have always wanted their face and name in as many places as possible; to that end, politicians in Victorian times supplied their constituents with plates, cups, knickknacks, and all sorts of textiles, all bearing the politicians' faces and names. Campaign fabric was often available of the same prints used to make handkerchiefs, and candidates also handed out campaign ribbons.

"Campaign ribbons were popular, inexpensive giveaways that kept the candidates fresh in the minds of voters," says G. Julie Powell in *The Fabric of Persuasion: Two Hundred Years of Political Quilts.* "Some men pinned [the ribbons] to their lapels; some wives and daughters saved them, often as bookmarks. The women could not vote, but they

Joke motto postcards were a popular item in the early twentieth century. Here a postcard circa 1920 rests against a circa 1910 Crazy quilt block. (Collection of the author. Photograph by Teressa Mahoney, Forever Yours Photography.)

I would like to have your Photograph——— For the center piece in my new crazy quilt.

Fraternal Order of Eagles (F.O.E.) and Veterans of Foreign Wars (V.F.W.) ribbons like these were favored not only for Crazy quilts, but for ribbon pillows and other parlor display items as well. (Photograph by Teressa Mahoney, Forever Yours Photography.)

could make crazy quilts, and when that time came, the ribbons were pulled from bibles and other books in fine condition, as they had been protected from light and wear."

Many of the campaign ribbons, like those promoting a particular cause or side during times of war, utilized patriotic motifs. Flags and eagles were especially popular symbols of patriotism, though faces of leaders like Abraham Lincoln and George Washington also came to be used this way. Catchy phrases and patriotic color schemes contributed to the ribbons' graphic quality and encouraged family and friends to support their local soldiers and favorite candidates.

The sheer quantity of ribbons, bandannas, and other graphic textile items became enormous over the years. At least twenty different silk kerchief or bandana designs, as well as nearly two hundred styles of silk ribbons, were printed for the 1841 presidential campaign of William Henry Harrison and John Tyler (whose famous campaign moniker was "Tippecanoe and Tyler too"). And this was just one set of candidates in one presidential race! Unfortunately, most of these now-valuable items were of poor quality or were discarded after the campaign was over, especially if the favored candidate was not a winner.

James G. Blaine (1830–1893), a U.S. senator from Maine and two-time U.S. secretary of state, was the Republican candidate for the 1884 presidential election—but lost to Grover Cleveland. Pictured here are a campaign card and ribbon supporting Blaine. (Collection of the author. Photograph by Teressa Mahoney, Forever Yours Photography.)

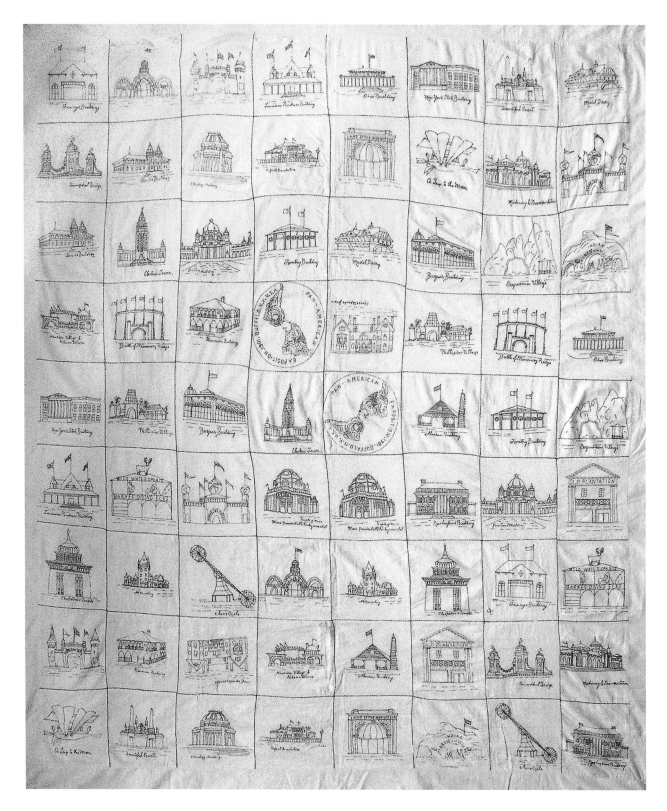

Pan-American Redwork cotton quilt top | Date: ca. 1901–1905 | Maker: Unknown | Size: 75" x 85"
Redwork-style patterns featuring the buildings and attractions of the Pan-American Exposition in Buffalo, New York, were sold as souvenirs. President William McKinley was shot while visiting the Pan-Am's Temple of Music on September 5, 1901; he died eight days later. Many Pan-Am quilts contain not only his image, but that of his successor, Theodore Roosevelt. (Collection of the author. Photograph by Teressa Mahoney, Forever Yours Photography.)

Transportation

Victorian Age transportation began with the horse and buggy (or wagon), but by the end of the nineteenth century, other forms were finding their place on Crazy quilts. The automobile was a major interest, but bicycles—one-wheeled velocipedes, as well as the more standard two-wheeled version—ships, hot air balloons, and more were represented.

When the transcontinental railroad was finally finished on May 10, 1869, in Promontory Point, Utah, it began affecting textile design and distribution. Early railroad designs were woven into linsey-woolsey-style coverlets in the 1850s and appliquéd on borders of patchwork quilts before 1869. By the 1880s, they were being stitched on Crazy quilts, too.

Related to the transportation theme was the map quilt. Pieced in Crazy fashion, a map quilt showed railroad lines and roads in aerial photograph style. One of the two known map quilts, now in the collection of the Newark Museum in New Jersey, was made by the wife of the Delaware, Lackawanna & Western Railroad superintendent.

Many of the designs for transportation motifs were traced or adapted directly from magazines and books; they do not seem to have been offered for sale in pattern form as frequently as other subjects.

Travel Memories

Going to a World's Fair? Bring back a ribbon, pillow cover, handkerchief, tablecloth, or a set of designs for embroidery that pictured exhibition buildings and popular events; many such souvenirs were incorporated into stitchers' needlework projects. Buildings and mottoes are included in Crazies, but more commonly in Redwork quilts. Embroidery pattern series were popular purchases at both the Columbus (1892–1893) and Pan American (1901–1902) expositions. (See "Politics and Patriotism" for more details on the latter.)

"Australian Memories" | Date: 2007 | Maker: Judith Baker Montano | Size: 26" x 33"
Every bit of the materials in this evocative rendition of the Land Down Under, from threads to fabric, was given to Judith by her Aussie students over twenty-two years of teaching. The hand-painted cottage painting, surrounded by a burnout shape of Australia, was inspired by a Queenslander home in High Gate Hill, Queensland. The border design was traced from actual gum leaves; kangaroos and koala bears add suitable touches. (Photograph courtesy of the quiltmaker)

THE FLAME BURNS LOW

Like all interests that burn bright and quickly, the Crazy quilt mania could not hold every member of its audience—especially those who prided themselves on following new trends, not old ones. Even as early as 1884, an editor at *Harper's Bazar* was dismissing Crazy quiltmakers as having "eaten of the insane root that takes reason prisoner. Their countless stitches and

Eventually the term "Crazy quilt" came to represent a comforting, if slightly offbeat mix. For centuries, the term has been applied to collections of stories or poems, music, even countries! Here are two twentieth-century versions: the 1931 Broadway revue Billy Rose's Crazy Quilt and L. Frank Baum's 1913 Patchwork Girl of Oz, a continuation of the Wizard of Oz series begun in 1900.

ugly ingenuity appear to them the fit expression of aesthetic instincts." By 1887, *Godey's Lady's Book*, which had praised Crazy patchwork to the skies, was dismissing it: "[T]he time, patience, stitches and mistakes the crazy quilt represents, are too awful for words." The *Godey's* editor harrumphed, "[W]e regretted much the time and energy spent on the most childish, and unsatisfactory of all work done with the needle, 'crazy' patch-work, and we strongly recommend that prizes for such work be omitted from all future announcements." Like the *Godey's* editor, other magazine editors were no longer even mentioning the Crazy in print, except in derision. (One wonders if this was partly because they themselves did not possess the skills needed to make a Crazy. Certainly many magazine writers and designers were not active quiltmakers—a fact that sometimes led to inaccurate patterns or awkward designs.) Cotton once again emerged as the quilt fabric of choice, although quilts in general were not considered technically interesting, except to those in rural areas or with limited means.

Crazy-quilt marketing probably had reached its saturation point, though related merchandise continued to be advertised and sold up through World War I. Related trends, like redwork and cigarette-silk accessories, were gaining in popularity; soon they would outdistance the Crazy in popularity, though never eclipse it entirely.

Although their popularity waned, Crazies continued to be made in large quantities through the early years of the new century. The Victorian silk Crazy was gradually supplanted by heavy wool Crazies (and woolen rectangle- or square-pieced comforters made from suit-fabric samples); these wool Crazies were made more frequently in rural areas than cosmopolitan ones. The cotton Crazy reemerged in the 1890s, probably encouraged by the resurrection of its sister, the traditional patchwork quilt, as an economical way to use up scraps for every day use. The turn of the nineteenth century also saw the rise of string piecing, a variation of the Log Cabin/Crazy piecing technique, which used strips and strings of leftover cotton fabrics stitched to a newspaper background. (Some consider this technique a Crazy method, though its patches tend to be more consistent in shape than those of the traditional Crazy.) Embroidery and embellishments adorned the wool Crazy, but rarely the cotton versions.

Cigarette silks, or tobacco silks as they were also called, were popular, colorful images silkscreened onto cotton or silk and included as free premiums in packs or cartons of cigarettes and cigars. These silks were collected and stitched into all sorts of decorative pieces, from pillows to lap quilts and Crazies. Many of these silks bore images of American flags and flags of other countries, a special boon for the new Americans who had immigrated only a few years before. Sometimes the flags were shown alone; more often, they were accompanied by images of animals, pretty girls, even musical scores of national anthems. Other themes on cigarette silks included Indian tribes (these silks are very collectible today), sports figures, U.S. presidents, kings and queens, fruit, flowers, crying babies, universities, soldiers, and actresses. Oddities were popular: one company, Zira, had silks depicting women with human heads and cigarettes for bodies. Whatever the theme or idea, there was probably a silk for it. Cigarette silks were available for purchase as a complete series or could be collected, pack by pack.

Cigar ribbons (fancy printed ribbons that tied up bundles of cigars) were also avidly collected and stitched into display pieces, including Crazies.

Cigarette silks were popular turn-of-the-century giveaways in cartons or packs of cigarettes and cigars. They could also be purchased separately as a series. These silks feature Austria (pretty girl included free of charge!) and China, both from Nebo, and an actress silk from Old Mill Cigarettes.

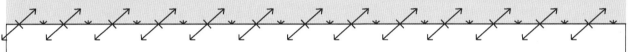

Crazies Unfinished

Many Crazy tops from the nineteenth and twentieth centuries never made it to the finishing stage. Instead, they were packed away, often for decades until young relatives grew up and suddenly discovered "Grandma's quilt" in the cedar chest. There seem to be several reasons for this.

Trends changed. The patient piecing, appliqué, and handwork of Crazy quilts often took several years to complete. By the time the top was finished, the quilt was no longer in style.

Quiltmakers could no longer go on. Unlike other quilt styles, Crazies were often the work of one person rather than a group. Age, sickness (including eye troubles, arthritis, and rheumatism), and death kept many quiltmakers from making their Crazy quilt tops into finished quilts—and many of the tops themselves were never completed.

Memories were too strong. By their nature, Crazies were repositories of memories, and many of those memories were associated with unpleasant events. Many a Crazy quilter probably put her top away "for now" (you wouldn't throw it away—too much work had gone into it!) and never again picked it up.

Funds were not available. The scraps or a purchased scrap bundle for piecing a Crazy top weren't too expensive, but the batting and backing required to finish the quilt were. In that case, the top might have put away to be finished when times weren't so hard.

But one of the strongest reasons for not finishing a Crazy top was something not in the quiltmaker's power. Lax manufacturing laws earlier in the nineteenth

Redwork-style pillow top | Date: ca. 1915 | Maker: Unknown | Size: 28" x 28"

Kits like this Redwork cross-stitched pillow top used the same bird motifs as those found on cigarette silks. The central eagle, silk-screened on a cotton background, gives the quilt a patriotic theme. (Collection of the author. Photograph by Teressa Mahoney, Forever Yours Photography.)

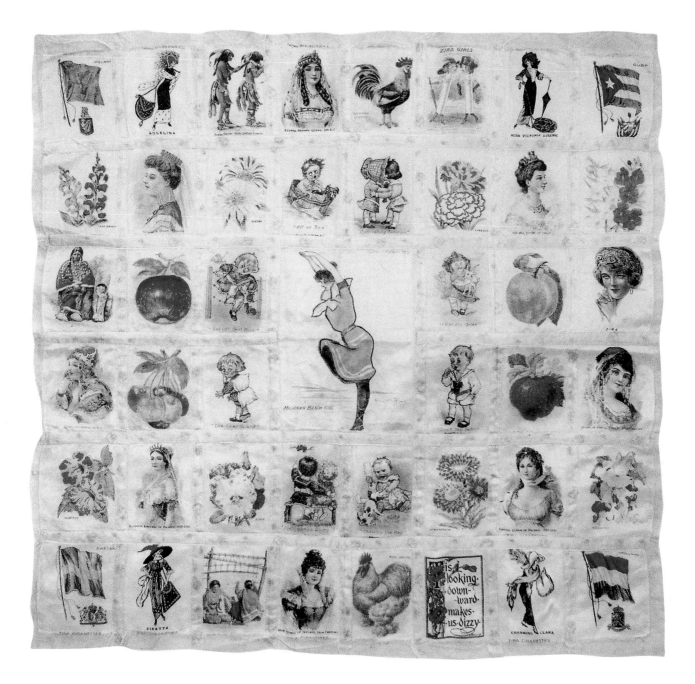

Cigarette Silk pillow top | Date: ca. 1910 | Maker: Unknown | Size: 24" x 24"

A wide variety of cigarette silks—featuring everything from bathing beauties to fruit, flowers, and even Indians and royalty—make up this appealing piece. Pink flowered silk ribbon, tacked in place, was used to outline each silk. (Collection of the author. Photograph by Teressa Mahoney, Forever Yours Photography.)

Unfinished Silk Crazy | Date: 1898 | Maker: Unknown | Size: 73" x 66½"

The spider web in the center of this quilt was an important motif for Victorian Crazy quilters. Spiders and their webs—in fact, any kind of bug—were an Oriental symbol for good luck and good fortune. Some circles hold that every Crazy quilt includes an embroidered spider web, but research shows that fan motifs are far more common. Note the floral painted squares, one in each corner; painting, like "art embroidery," was a hallmark of education and good breeding. Why was this quilt left unfinished? Perhaps the maker became sick or died. Or she realized that weighted silks were slowly destroying her hard work . . . and she no longer had an incentive to do more. (Minnesota Historical Society)

century allowed manufacturers to produce weighted silks. These were regular silk yardages soaked in various solutions, including iron, antimony, and sometimes even arsenic, until they absorbed up to five times their weight. Weighted silks were highly profitable; one yard of regular silk could, after being soaked, become five yards of saleable weighted silk. Weighted silks looked fine. They swished beautifully in fashionable skirts and ball gowns. And because they were cheap, they were sold in great quantities.

Unfortunately, they were also fragile. In less than a decade, weighted silks would start to break down, shred, and shatter, and there was no reasonable way to repair them. Many women purchased weighted silks for their Crazy quilting, and when their work began to pay the price, there was nothing they could do about it. Heartbroken, they would tuck the damaged quilt top away, promising themselves they'd eventually do something about the damage, but never did.

Weighted silks continue to be one of the antique Crazy quilt's greatest foes. The damage that began back in the 1800s has, in many cases, continued today. The continued shredding and splitting eventually destroys the patch, then the patch next to it, until the quilt is too tattered to be preserved. Some techniques have been developed to help slow down the destruction, including protecting the area with a basted covering of netting or Crepoline (a sheer fabric used to protect damaged areas). Restoration-quality fusibles help in stabilizing these weakened areas, as well. But these Crazies would have been far better off if weighted silks had never been invented. Weighted silks still exist today, but are now have to be labeled as such.

At the turn of the twentieth century, Crazies used art silks, woven from an artificial fiber invented from coal tar in 1885. These art silks became so popular that their price eclipsed that of the real silk. But weighted silks remained a problem, and many fabrics from the early part of the twentieth century, especially silks, continued to have problems with colorfastness.

CRAZIES IN THE TWENTIETH CENTURY

By the advent of World War I, Crazy quilters had retreated into the woodwork, except for those dedicated few who quietly continued to stitch and embroider the patterns they loved best. Crazies were rarely shown in magazines, except for an antique feature now and then.

The 1930s brought a new interest in all kinds of patchwork, including the overlooked Crazy. Some of the interest was out of necessity; the Great Depression had decimated incomes, and families still needed to be kept warm. Wool crazies were stitched from old scraps, including military uniforms; rectangle- and square-pieced coverlets, some made from suit samples, resurfaced as well. Cotton Crazy tops were resurrected to be tied and finished into warm quilts. The latter trend became so strong that cotton "cheater Crazy" prints, commercial fabrics in patterns designed to look like a finished patchwork print, became popular for backing these turn-of-the-century tops!

QUILTING CRAZY IN MODERN TIMES

The years following the Great Depression were rather quiet for any form of quilting, including the Crazy. The reasons for this slowdown are varied. For one, people who had grown up with quilts during hard times tended to associate them with those periods. When manufacturers produced inexpensive blankets in cheerful patterns and colors, many purchased them instead of going to the trouble of making a quilt. (Their foremothers would have been horrified at the amount of scraps simply thrown away!) Secondly, more women began working away from the home, giving them increased funds for buying decorative items and less time and energy for making them. And Crazies, with their tendency toward embellishments and embroidery, demanded even more time than the average project. Finally, textile arts, like other decorative movements, have their ups and downs in interest. The trend for quilting was down. Crazy quilts became a curiosity, still admired but rarely produced.

Continued on page 85

Great-Grandma's Woolen Crazies | Date: ca. 1890 | Makers: Mary Fuller Vincent Brown and Charlotte Fuller | Size: each 70" x 80"

Mary Vincent Brown was a Michigan farmwife; her sister Charlotte was a frequent visitor to the household. Mary and Charlotte made two woolen quilts, using leftovers from family sewing. They added a few luxurious touches—silk velvets and embroidery threads, probably saved for with Mary's egg money.

One comforter was used by the family. The other was carefully packed away, most likely in Charlotte's hope chest, and never used. (Charlotte never married.) Mary's daughter, Ethel Brown Cumings, inherited the heavily worn quilt after Mary's death in 1917. Charlotte gave Ethel the other comforter sometime before her own death in 1942. The two quilts were eventually passed down to Ethel's granddaughter, with instructions that they would always be kept together. (Collection of the author. Photograph by Mellisa Karlin Mahoney.)

"The Industry Quilt" | Date: 1918–1924 | Maker: Alice Beghtol Curtis | Size: 74" x 90"

Alice Curtis lived in the small town of Industry, Illinois, her entire life. Rural Illinois had no available electricity during this period; Alice must have made this entire Crazy by candle or kerosene light! We know little more about this amazing quiltmaker, except that she had no children, and her husband Oscar, according to community gossip, was not an easy man to live with. According to Oscar, Alice made this quilt in six years, finishing it in 1924 (the date on the quilt). She used wool fabrics, a common (and economical) choice for rural housewives, but unusual for a quilt of this complexity and workmanship. She did her embroidering with wool darning thread. Some of the names and initials embroidered include "Everet," "Gerda Hammon," "B. C.," and "N. P." Alice also made other quilts, but no one is quite sure what happened to them. When she died in 1936, aged seventy-eight, the funeral director took this quilt in payment for her funeral. (Photograph courtesy of Joan Stevens, American Doodah)

Right middle: *"The Industry Quilt," bottom center, urn detail. Alice Curtis did not have an easy life, but she lavished detail and fine workmanship on this astonishing wool quilt. (Photograph courtesy of Joan Stevens, American Doodah)*

Right bottom: *Alice Beghtol Curtis (1858–1936) of Industry, Illinois. (Photograph courtesy of Joan Stevens, American Doodah)*

FAMOUS DESIGNS FROM OLD PATCHWORK QUILTS

New Versions of the Crazy Quilt

75

1783

1818

75

No. 1818. The "Star Block" and "Cactus Basket"—both old designs, are beautifully adapted for quilt making with modern materials. The Cactus Basket may be made entirely of patch pieces or have alternate plain blocks. Two quilting designs are given in the pattern, which states amount of material required. Quilts can be made single or double bed size. Pattern, 35 cents.

No. 1783. The "Windmill" and "Snowball" quilts —designed to be made by machine. But, of course, they're lovely of handwork, too. The Snowball quilt is charming of white combined with a white figured print. The Windmill is effective in a print, plain color and white. Pattern states the materials required. Single or double bed sizes. Pattern, 30 cents.

No. 75. New versions of the famous Crazy Quilt—that stand-by of Colonial days. The one pieced of long rectangular sections might be made of old neckties. A crazy quilt in a flower design is shown just below this. And, just above, you see the feather stitched crazy quilt, but made in blocks so it's easier for you to handle. Blocks are 12 to 14 ins. square. Pattern, 30 cents.

Depression-era magazines usually featured patchwork and appliqué blocks; getting the actual pattern often required sending a nickel, dime, or quarter to the magazine. The Crazy (bottom right) however, like the Log Cabin (top left), needed no special pattern and used up small scraps—an invaluable trait during hard times.

Crazy cheater print, three versions: the original circa 1884 print, somewhat faded (bottom right); the 1997 "Vintage Spirit" reproduction by Kaye England (top right); and the Bicentennial version (top left). (Pillow/crib top from the collection of Mary Ghormley, rest from the collection of the author. Photograph by Teressa Mahoney, Forever Yours Photography.)

Continued from page 81

Americans' attitude toward quilting gradually began to rise as the country moved toward its Bicentennial in 1976. (Coincidentally, the Crazy's other period of affluence came exactly a century earlier, at America's Centennial in 1876.) *McCall's Needlework and Crafts Bicentennial Quilt Book*, published in 1975, began by saying, "Americans have never stopped making quilts—from colonial days, when every bit of cloth was precious, right on up to now. Some of those quilts [are] . . . gathered together . . . to be admired anew, then reinterpreted in today's materials."

Since many of "today's materials" were artificial fibers, it is tempting to say that they were invented only in the mid-twentieth century. It is true that many mid-twentieth-century fiber innovations came during the wartime search for a cheaper substitute for parachute silk. However, the first artificial fiber, eventually known as art silk, was invented in the 1880s, using coal tar and artificial spinnerets that mimicked the way spiders spin webs. For a time in the early twentieth century, interest in (and the price of) art silks surpassed that of the real thing! Rayons, which had been invented in 1894, were on the market by 1910, though not called by that name until 1924.

These old/new fibers were joined in Crazy quilts with polyester, a 1941 invention, and its cousin, Dacron, in 1950. Ultrasuede made its appearance in 1970, just in time to become a fabric choice for Crazies, as well. Other lesser-known fibers also began to appear.

The Bicentennial-era Crazy, in some ways, looked very much like its late-Victorian ancestors, incorporating the same velvets and other fancy fabrics, lots of embroidery, and ribbons. But quiltmakers mixed the new fibers with the old. Velvets were more apt to be woven from polyester blends, rather than silk. Hand painting gave way to commercially stamped and printed images. And embroidery, though still used to outline patches and embroider the occasional image, was done with other floss than just silk.

The Smithsonian's National Museum of American History stores its quilts and other textiles in a temperature- and moisture-controlled "clean room." Each drawer holds one or more pieces; the one pulled out features a Victorian-era Crazy with a tasseled-edge border. Don't miss the nineteenth-century Mosaic above it, as well. (Author's visit to the Smithsonian. Photograph by Marsha Brick.)

The modern Crazy quilt, like quilting in general, was again on the radar of the modern world, fueled by a number of small but interrelated events in the last quarter of the twentieth century. Bonnie Leman, a Denver-area schoolteacher, began *Quilter's Newsletter Magazine* in her basement, typing on carbon stencils. The first issue, September 1969, featured a mix of modern and antique quilts. Two years later, a young couple who collected Amish quilts, Jonathan Holstein and Gail Van der Hoof, curated an exhibit, "Abstract Design in American Quilts," for the Whitney Museum of American Art in New York City—the first time anyone had presented quilts as wall graphics. This concept rocked the art world and began a movement to consider quilts, both antique and new, from a different viewpoint than the utilitarian one.

Other events contributing to the Crazy resurgence include the 1972 publication of *America's Quilts and Coverlets* by Carleton L. Safford and Robert Bishop, a dealer who was the curator of the Henry Ford Museum in Michigan. (Eventually Bishop, who frequently featured quilts, including Crazies, in his books on folk art, became the director of the American Folk Art Museum.) In 1975, Bishop followed with *New Discoveries in American Quilts*, which included a chapter primarily on Crazies.

Many prominent collectors began their work in the 1970s, including Robert and Ardis James, who bought their first quilt in 1979 and eventually donated the lion's share of their mammoth collection to the International Quilt Study Center in Lincoln, Nebraska. Joel and Kate Kopp began gathering quilts, including many unusual Crazies, for their shop, American Hurrah, in New York City. Shelly Zegart actively collected quilts and in 1981, along with Eleanor Bingham Miller, began the Kentucky Quilt Project, a state documentation that spawned similar projects in dozens of states. Many antique quilts, including Crazies, were brought out for examination and recording on state databases.

Anything quilt-related suddenly became newsworthy. Crazy quilts certainly benefited from this new interest, especially the 1984 publication of *Crazy Quilts*, written by art curator Penny McMorris, who had published a book on American patchwork design for the BBC only a few years before. (She was also known for her 1981 public television series *Quilting with Penny McMorris*; one segment was devoted entirely to the Crazy quilt.) McMorris's book was the first to present Crazy quilting not only from a historical context, but also an artistic one. She combined antique quilts and paper ephemera, like postcards, ads, and trade cards, with modern Crazy photos from artists such as Gail Fraas and Duncan Slade. McMorris was catching the new approach to Crazies, and quilts in general, that took hold in the 1980s: viewing textiles as art. Terrie Hancock

Continued on page 90

Crazy | Date: 1889 | Maker: Mary T.H. Willard | Size: 83" x 67"

Mary Willard had plenty to say on this unusual embroidered wool Crazy made of suiting, serge, and wool gabardine fabrics. Often quilts of this style feature quotes from the Bible, as well as popular sayings of the time. (International Quilt Study Center at the University of Nebraska–Lincoln, 1997.007.0318)

Cotton Multi-Generation Tied Crazy | Date: ca. 1890
and 1935 | Maker: Unknown | Size: 72" x 80"
*In the 1930s, someone used a Crazy cheater print to back and
finish a turn-of-the-century quilt top. Many of these duo-period
Crazies were made for warmth as well as decorative purposes.
(Collection of the author. Photographs by Teressa Mahoney,
Forever Yours Photography.)*

Tie Crazy | Date: ca. 1955 | Maker: Unknown | Size: 75" x 82"
Rayons, polyesters, and other artificial fibers were developed during wartime, often as a possible substitute for silks, which were used in parachutes and other applications. Within a decade of each war's end (especially World War II), these new fabrics would appear on the popular market. This 1950s quiltmaker mixed a variety of polyester and rayon ties (from her husband, perhaps?) with—of all things—a 1953 bank bag! The backing is a slippery, light blue, synthetic satin. (Collection of the author. Photographs by Teressa Mahoney, Forever Yours Photography.)

Continued from page 86
Mangat, Michael James, Nancy Crow, and others added strip-pieced details in their work, which was often inspired by or imitated a Crazy-style look. (Strip piecing is a process of cutting strips, sewing them together, then recutting them for a new look. It became especially popular with the appearance of the rotary cutter tool.) Mangat's entry for "The Art Quilt," a 1986 traveling exhibit by McMorris and Rod Kiracofe, included a Crazy-pieced background and all sorts of beads, buttons, and other small objects—a piece that not only reawakened interest in embellishing, but also made Mangat famous for it. Her "Dashboard Saints" gained even more attention when *The Art Quilt*, a book/show catalog, was published by McMorris and Michael Kile the same year.

"The air was full of excitement and experimentation," writes Robert Shaw, curator of the Shelburne Museum in Shelburne, Vermont, in his essay "Five Decades of Unconventional Quilts: The 1980s." "The trailblazers of the '80s were not only ambitious in their art, but also in their desire for recognition. They wanted to be seen as artists, not quiltmakers, and they wanted their work accepted as art both within the quilt and in the larger world of fine art collecting . . . They knew they faced an uphill battle, but they were totally committed to their art and determined to wage it anyway." (Shaw has written his own books on folk art and textiles, including antique and art quilts.)

The Quilt Digest, a yearly journal devoted both old and new quilts, began publishing in 1983 and continued on for several years, thanks to Kiracofe and his partner, Michael Kile, a San Francisco quilt dealer. Many Crazy quilts appeared in the *Quilt Digest's* issues, often contrasted with modern quilts in the same article. Kiracofe saw this blending as critical; both he and Kile wanted the periodical "to be a bridge for the antique quilt world to really look at, [and] begin to understand and appreciate the works being done today."

A young Canadian-born artist named Judith Baker Montano was watching all these changes with her own brand of excitement. Accomplished in both paint and pencil art, she began a quilt when her son was born. "I decided that it was time," she later

Terrie Hancock Mangat is considered by many to have jump-started modern interest in quilting embellishments. Terrie's quilts use a wide variety of beads, bits, and found objects, and vary from string and Crazy-style piecing to appliquéd "memory jars" (one of her specialties) and other memorials. Terrie lives in Valdez, New Mexico. (Photograph courtesy of Terrie Hancock Mangat)

remembered in her book, *Art & Inspirations*. "The women on my father's side were all known for their beautiful needlework and quilts. My mother was also a wizard with any type of needlework and sewing, but somehow these talents held no interest for me until my son was born. I was a late bloomer, and at the age of twenty-six, I finally began my love affair with needle and thread."

Several traditional pieced quilts later, including some prizewinning strip-pieced designs, she felt frustrated. "Somehow, the thousands of stitches I made never really satisfied all my interests," she wrote in *Crazy Quilt Odyssey*. "Being told to confine my fabric purchases to 100% cotton [a common instruction in quilting then] was a painful handicap, especially with all those luscious satins, silks, and polyesters tempting me from the very next aisle . . . They called out to the gypsy in my soul!"

The frustrated artist became a writer, designer, and teacher—and one of modern Crazy quilting's most influential people. "At last, here was a technique
Continued on page 94

"Dashboard Saints: In Memory of Saint Christopher (Who Lost His Magnetism)" | Date: 1985 | Maker: Terrie Hancock Mangat | Size: 123" x 99"

"Dashboard Saints" was made especially for the three-year traveling exhibit *The Art Quilt* (1986), curated by Michael Kile, founder of the *Quilt Digest*, and Penny McMorris. The quilt was one of the first to bring Terrie's work to national attention, for its innovative mix of appliqué, embellishment, and patchwork. "I had this extremely intense Catholic upbringing," Terrie says. "About the time I made that quilt, the church was going through a lot of change. They reviewed the list of saints, and they decided certain saints weren't really saints. They couldn't prove that they ever existed, so they deleted them from the list of sainthood. . . . I had on my car all these little plastic [magnetic] dashboard saints . . . [the Saint Christopher figure] fell on the ground. That's when I started thinking about that. Saint Christopher was deleted, he lost his magnetism." Another "deleted" favorite, Saint Valentine, is also included in the quilt. (Photographs courtesy of the quiltmaker)

"Cleveland Fireworks" | Date: 1993 | Maker: Terrie Hancock Mangat | Size: 72" x 120"

Fireworks splatter across the surface of this strip-pieced art quilt, installed in the entrance foyer of the Cleveland University Hospital in Ohio. Terrie used diagonal stitching and bright white "explosions" in the foreground to emphasize the bright colors of the background and give the quilt a three-dimensional feel. (Photograph courtesy of the quiltmaker)

Judith Baker Montano is a modern quilting pioneer. Her 1980s books on Crazy techniques and embellishments, especially her piecing techniques and work in silk-ribbon embroidery, permanently changed how modern quilters approached Crazy quilting. Originally from near the Canadian Rockies in Alberta, Canada, Judith now lives in La Veta, Colorado. (Photograph courtesy of Judith Baker Montano)

ABOVE AND OPPOSITE: **"Sea Garden"** | Date: 2006 | Maker: Judith Baker Montano | Size: 20" x 27"
Judith's newfound love of scuba diving and snorkeling on the Great Barrier Reef in Australia inspired this multi-textured piece, which includes netting, beads, ribbons, fish, and shell buttons and findings. The embellishments were created with freeform embroidery, ruching, and tucking techniques, or by burning and melting layers. (Photographs courtesy of the quiltmaker)

Continued from page 90

that would let me be an artist," she later wrote in *Art & Inspirations*. "I could finally mix fabrics together simply because they pleased me. Lush colors in satin, silk, velvet, calico, lace and wool—they were all there to be used like paint on a palette." After approaching a teacher who dismissed Crazy quilting as "not worth bothering with," Montano taught herself, adding her own piecing and embroidery methods to the traditional ones she learned. (She credits not only Penny McMorris's book as a great influence on her during this period, but also Dorothy Bond's *Crazy Quilt Stitches*, a 1981 self-published book of stitches copied from antique quilts that became a perennial classic.)

When Montano wasn't making Crazy quilts, or working as a curator in the Denver Art Museum's textile department, she began teaching. One of her early venues was the International Quilt Festival in Houston, Texas, where she still teaches regularly. Besides working in the United States, she spent many years teaching in Australia and Japan, which not only influenced her personal style (and others in the process), but spread interest in Crazy quilting to those countries, as well.

Montano's first book, *The Crazy Quilt Handbook*, was published in 1986. In the coming decades, she wrote several more Crazy-related books, including stitching guides for punch needle and silk ribbon embroidery with a floral theme—another trend originally powered by her that has since spread to many Crazy teachers and designers. Montano was one of the first Crazy artists to

introduce Western, Southwestern, and Native American themes in her work, inspired in part by her mixed heritage of several different cultures. She was one of the first artists to popularize piecing and embellishing landscapes and other natural themes, as well as the more traditional-looking Victorian style of Crazy quilt.

It is difficult to summarize Montano's many contributions to the themes and trends that influence modern Crazy quilters—there are too many! Other teachers and artists have also contributed to the modern art of Crazy quilting; like Montano, many worked on their own quilts for decades before they began teaching and writing about quilting. During Crazy quilting's rise to national (and international) prominence in the late 1980s and early 1990s, these teachers were in great demand. They included Betty Pillsbury, whose work won several national awards; Australian Gloria McKinnon of Anne's Glory Box; Leslie Levison, whose work sometimes experimented with mermaid or motorcycle themes; and Christine Dabbs, whose skillful Japanese-style embroidery and Crazies for the 1995 movie *How to Make an American Quilt* pushed her into national prominence. (Dabbs published her classic *Crazy Quilting*, based on her techniques and experiences with the movie, in 2000.) Other teachers include Charlotte Angotti, Nancy Eha, Rosemary Eichorn, Jane Hall, Dixie Haywood, and Barbara Randle, to name but a few.

A number of these teachers continue to find their voice—and audience—at the Crazy Quilt Society (CQS), the first worldwide group devoted primarily to Crazy quilting. CQS, as it is known, was founded by Nancy and Bill Kirk. Their business, the Kirk Collection, specialized in antique and reproduction fabrics, for both the stitcher and the quilt restorer; in fact, the Kirks had supplied textiles old and new for several movies and television series, including *Quantum Leap*. In 1995, they began a special newsletter, the *Crazy Quilt Support Group*, for their many customers requesting materials for use in Crazies. (Nancy herself was an accomplished Crazy quilter and restorer who often taught classes.)

"Initially the Support Group focused on historic Crazy quilts and vintage fabrics and trims," Nancy remembered in a recent personal interview. "But it soon became apparent that contemporary Crazy quilters wanted more. So I started the Crazy Quilt Society under the umbrella of the non-profit Quilt Heritage Foundation." The first conference was held in Omaha, Nebraska, in 1998; one of CQS's first teachers was Camille Dalphond Cognac, a quilt collector and teacher who also specialized in restoring and repairing Crazy quilts. Her *Quilt Restoration: A Practical Guide* (1994) has become a classic. (Cognac, along with the Kirks, founded the Quilt Restoration Society, also under the auspices of Quilt Heritage Foundation; the Quilt Restoration Guild takes its place, as of this writing.)

For more than a decade, Crazy quilters have met in Omaha for an annual conference. "It became a place for Crazy quilters who met online to get together face-to-face," Nancy says. "The conference features national and regional teachers, vendors, exhibits, and special events like the Prom Dress Swap [a favorite since year one] and the Great Fiber Exchange." As of this writing, the Crazy Quilt Society remains the world's largest group of Crazy aficionados, including writers, stitchers, teachers, designers, and restorers. As interest in embellishments continued to grow throughout the 1990s and the new century, beaders and embroiders have joined the group and continue to broaden its interests. Other groups, like the Embroiderers Guild of America, as well as many informal groups across the world, continue to educate and inspire each other.

In recent years, collectors and stitchers have renewed interest in Crazies, both as objects of admiration and as personal challenges for those who want to learn a new skill. "Crazy quilts have always fascinated me," Montano writes. "What other handcraft combines embroidery, sewing, appliqué, laces, ribbons, buttons, beading, painting and color design? Though other crafts may distract me, I am always drawn back to beautiful, outrageous crazy quilts. They remind me of mysterious, glittering jewels, like gypsy cousins peeking out from a patchwork of traditional sister quilts."

May this book be your first step—or a continuation of your walk—along the fascinating path of Crazy quilts.

"Morning Glorious" (detail) | Date: 2006 | Maker: Judith Baker Montano | Size: 22" x 34"
This Crazy quilt collage shares Judith's love of morning glory flowers, using layers of silk ribbon work, beading, embroidery stitches, and antique buttons. (Collection of Mr. and Mrs. Brad Jackson. Photograph courtesy of the quiltmaker.)

"All Things Old Are New Again" | Date: 1998 | Maker: Nancy Eha | Size: 30" x 18"
The unusual "Crazy beading" technique featured on this piece is one of Nancy Eha's trademarks. It looks like traditional embroidery stitching—but is done entirely with beads, instead! (Photograph courtesy of the quiltmaker)

PART TWO

HOW TO MAKE A CRAZY QUILT

Hopefully the quilts in this book have inspired you to start your own Crazy quilt. One of the best facets of quiltmaking is its versatility. Although there are all sorts of pronouncements about the "proper" or "best" way to make a pattern, the truth is that all sorts of quilts can be stitched using all sorts of methods. Some are faster, some are not. Some use a sewing machine, others rely on handwork. Crazy quilts are no exception to this rule.

PLANNING YOUR QUILT

Before you get started on your Crazy, ask yourself:

- What kind of use do I plan for this quilt? (Will it be a bed quilt, wall hanging, table runner, piece of clothing, baby quilt, or something else?)
- What size would I like to make?
- How much time do I have?
- Do I want to wash this piece?

Your answers to these questions will help you decide the following:

What Fabric Should I Use?

If you're envisioning a quilt or pillow rich with silk velvets, woven jacquard ribbons, beautifully woven damasks and so on—these are not perfect choices for a baby's crib! For one thing, "fancy" fabrics like satins, embossed velvets, and Chinese silks do not wash well; most are meant to be dry-cleaned. One "urpy" session will put your lovely quilt permanently out of commission! (Also, Baby will have a wonderful time pulling off and swallowing the buttons, charms, and other memorabilia you have so painstakingly added, so save embellishments for other Crazies that will stay away from children's hands.)

If your Crazy is meant for display and careful use, consider using fancier fabrics—they're perfect for the job. But for a piece that will need to endure more abuse and/or washing, concentrate on more washable fabrics, especially cottons. Don't leave out silks—many of these are washable, but double-check. Prints, solids, textures, weaves, and especially batiks—these are all perfect for Crazy quiltmaking. Many woven ribbons, lace, and trims are washable, too, but check first.

OPPOSITE: Judith Baker Montano's work, like this quilt detail, layers not only different fabrics, but also embellishments like photo transfers and silk ribbon for a rich, multi-textured look. (Photograph courtesy of the quiltmaker)

A boy sits on the counter in a dry-goods shop, likely in the Midwest circa 1890. These shops stocked bolts of fabrics for dresses and quilts, as well as thread, laces, buttons, and more. Many had pattern catalogs for redwork and embroidery; for a short time in the early 1900s, one penny purchased a quilt square marked with a pattern ready for embroidering.

It is helpful to remember that many of the fabric terms we know well, like *velvet*, *satin*, and *brocade*, are actually references to how the fabric is woven or patterned. These fancy fabrics can use any number of fibers, including natural ones like silk and wool, or artificial ones, like rayon. Velvets, for example, can be woven from silk, wool, cotton, and artificial fibers. (If there's a linen-based velvet out there, I've never heard of it.)

A surprising amount of these fabrics are washable to some degree. Most demand special care and/or hand washing, though. You'll get best results from firmly woven fabrics that don't shift around too much.

Tip: Clear out your treasured bits and pieces. Do you have a bit of lace, an old quilt block, Grandma's embroidered hand towel, a hankie you couldn't bear to throw out? These textile odds and ends are perfect additions to your Crazy quilt. Not only will they be preserved in usable form, but they'll also add a timeless sense of history to your work. Damaged items are excellent candidates—just cut around the area to be used, adding approximately $\frac{1}{2}$ inch for seam allowances.

Tip: Adapt the materials to the quilt's planned use. If you're going to use the quilt on the bed every night, be sure to use fabrics that can stand long-term wear, especially cottons, washable silks, or artificial fibers. Also, keep family members from sitting, lying, or doing their study lessons (with a ballpoint pen!) on top of the quilt. (I mention this from sad experience.)

Tip: Check fabric for colorfastness. Here's an easy way. Lightly dampen a cotton swab or cotton ball. Brush it across the fabric or other item in question. If any color shows on the cotton, the fabric is going to bleed some of that dye when washed. (If you're not planning on washing your finished quilt, colorfastness won't be a problem. If you are, it will. Either wash the fabric until it no longer runs color, or set the dye by soaking it in a large bowl of water and a handful of salt. There are products on the market to help with this, too.)

A plethora of fabrics appears in this crazy-patched quilt on the cover of The Book of Patchwork, published by Woman's World Magazine Company in 1929.

How Much Fabric Should I Get?

For every 12 to 16 inches of Crazy quilt surface, you'll need approximately ²/₃ yard of various scraps. (For smaller-sized scraps, add another ¹/₃ yard for safety's sake.) Don't forget scraps of lace, netting, and chiffon—they can be used to add another interesting layer to the finished piece. You'll also want to use lengths of lace and woven trim; 10- to 12-inch cuts minimum should give you plenty to work with. Buy 3 to 4 yards of trim or lace if you think you'll be using them for a border accent.

In the earliest days, because fabrics were expensive and hard to obtain, Crazy patchwork was done without a fabric foundation. However, your work will last longer if, like Victorian and later quilters, you make use of a fabric foundation. You'll need a piece of firmly woven fabric to use as foundation: the size of your finished quilt top, plus 5 to 10 inches extra all around. If you're making a large quilt comprising several Crazy patches sewn together, you will end up cutting your foundation into several units. Plan for at least 2 to 3 yards for a wall hanging. Plain sugar or flour sacks, or leftover fabrics were traditional choices for background fabrics. I'm particularly fond of white-on-white texture prints or cotton nonprints, but changeable satins or damask napkin-type fabrics are lovely, too. Muslin works well for bed-size quilts. (In the Victorian era, scrap paper or newsprint was sometimes used as background, but due to its acid content, it could and did damage the fabrics in the long run.) You can follow your ancestors' lead, and use leftover scrap fabrics as foundations, too.

While you're at it, you'll also need backing fabric for the back of the finished quilt. Polished cottons, velvets, and lightweight wools add an elegant touch; cottons wear well. Plan for a piece the size of your finished top, plus 4 inches extra all the way around. You'll also need 1 yard of binding fabric, cut in 2¹/₂-inch strips and joined together vertically.

What About a Bed-Sized Quilt?

Because of their bulk and embroidered areas, the vast majority of larger-sized Crazy quilts are made by joining a variety of square or rectangular units. (Sometimes diamond- or wedge-shaped units are substituted.) The traditional method is to stitch the units together without sashing or any other joining fabrics, then to embroider over the joined seams to camouflage them. Later twentieth-century Crazies often include sashing in between the blocks. Sashing, like an outer border, made the finished quilt larger with only a little more effort. Solid colors, often in fancy fabrics or polished cotton, make beautiful sashing and help stabilize the embroidered blocks.

If you are making a bed-sized piece, you'll need approximately 9 to 11 yards of various sized scraps, as well as 10 yards of a background foundation fabric. To decide on your quilt size, measure the length and width of your bed, including the top and sides. (Add 10 inches to the length if you like to tuck the quilt over your pillows.) Use this figure to decide on the size of your individual units (blocks, rectangles, or strips) and how many individual units you need.

Tip: Draw a rough sketch of your proposed quilt. Keep it in a handy place for reference. Nothing fancy here—just block units, sashing, and borders to help remember the overall layout. (This works well for other patchwork styles, too.) For more help with this and other general quiltmaking techniques, try Marianne Fons and Liz Porter's *The Quilter's Complete Guide*.

Tip: Include a border on your planned quilt. One or more borders will help protect your quilt from wear and tear every time you make the bed. A plain border can take the stress of pulling and tugging much more effectively than your Crazy-pieced blocks. It will also decrease the number of units needed to make your quilt—a real time saver. Plan for 2 to 3 yards. (To figure exact fabric, consult Fons and Porter's book, mentioned above.)

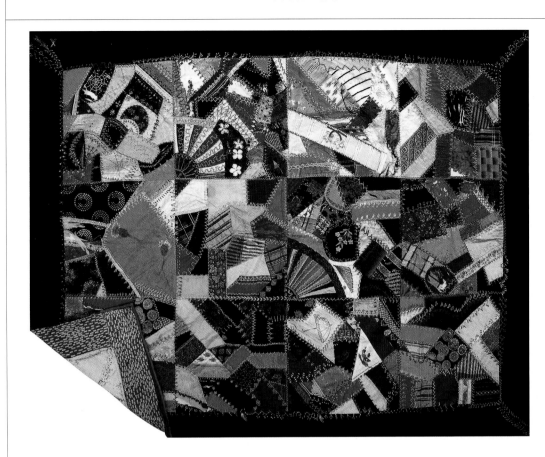

"To Tommy" Crazy top | Date: ca. 1885, 1915 | Maker: Unknown | Size: 60" x 72"

Sometime in the 1880s, the blocks in this top were pieced, but the quiltmaker did not join them until about 1915, when she added a twentieth-century velvet border backed with an Art Deco–style blue print. Her embroidery skills are impeccable; note the floral and umbrella details. The only clue to her identity is a penciled note on the quilt back: "To Tommy from Grandma." (Collection of the author. Photograph by Teressa Mahoney, Forever Yours Photography.)

CUTTING THE BACKGROUND FOUNDATION

Figure what size your background foundation needs to be, then add ¹⁄₂ inch on each side for seam allowances. For example, if you are planning to make a 20-inch square Crazy, you'll need to cut the foundation to be 20¹⁄₂ x 20¹⁄₂ inches.

For best results, cut your background fabric units slightly larger than you want them to be. Crazy patchwork units often end up smaller than their pre-pieced size, due to stitching shrinkage, so add at least 1 inch extra to your planned unit size. This extra inch also gives you enough room to trim the unit to the planned size when you've finished, giving you more accurate results.

Tip: If you are making a smaller-sized project, like a wall hanging or pillow, you can piece your Crazy in one big section, instead of a series of units. If you use a full width of fabric, say 40 to 44 inches, though, there is a tendency for the background fabric blocks to buckle in the middle. And that may lead to the fabric becoming wrinkled or shifting as you stitch. I personally would recommend stitching a section no larger than 21 inches square or long. Otherwise, I'd split the area needed into smaller units to be joined later.

THREE CONSTRUCTION METHODS

Use one of the following methods to stitch your Crazy. If making a larger quilt, such as a bed-size, piece each individual unit one at a time, adding embroidery and embellishments as you like.

Step One: *Stitch one patch onto another.*

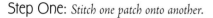

Step One, in fabric.

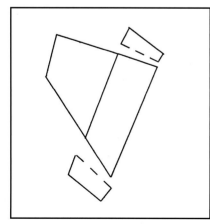

Step Two: *Trim and press back.*

---

1. The Basic Crazy: Traditional Method for Machine or Hand Piecing

The following method, used for centuries, is by far the most popular way to piece a Crazy quilt.

Materials

- For your background, a piece of firm-woven fabric, cut to the size of your finished unit plus $1\frac{1}{2}$". (See "Cutting the Background Foundation.")
- A variety of fabric scraps, including silks, wools, artificial fibers, or cottons. (See the earlier note on colorfastness if you want to wash your quilt.) Don't forget sheers, lace, or netting that can be layered over heavier fabrics for interesting effects.
- Any special items you plan to include—photo transfers, old bits and pieces of household linens, blocks, and so on.
- Lace, woven trims, tatting, and so on for trim.
- Cotton or silk sewing thread. Silk is best with handwork. It's more expensive, but it visually disappears into the fabric with each stitch. And it's strong.

> **Tip:** Try an experimental block first. Use scraps from other projects for stitching. This "study piece" will help you master the technique without worrying about waste.

Directions

Follow the same steps whether you stitch by machine or hand. But if using a machine, you'll want neutral-colored thread in both needle and bobbin. (I prefer cream or gray.) Your bobbin should be full. For hand sewing, use a needle you're comfortable with. (I prefer a quilting between, generally size 9 or 10.)

Work in a clean, well-lit place so you can see clearly what you're doing. If stitching by hand, try working on a slanted board or other flat surface, to minimize backaches from bending over your work.

Step One: Lay out your background fabric and smooth it flat. Choose a fabric scrap for your first piece and position in the unit's center. (Sometimes stitchers prefer to start from one of the sides. You'll want to experiment to see which area you like best.) A photo transfer or an embroidered section is a good item to feature; position it in place on the background fabric. If you're unsure on placement, try it in the middle.

Step Two, in fabric.

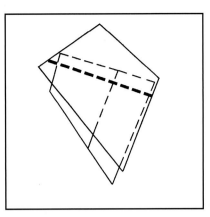

Step Three: *Add another patch.*

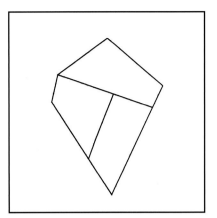

Step Four: *Trim and press back.*

Choose a second, contrasting fabric scrap; for ease, try one that has edges slightly longer than the first one, as shown in the diagram. Lay the second scrap on top of the first so that the front sides of both pieces of fabric are facing ("kissing each other," as kids would say), then stitch. Use an even running stitch if stitching by hand, or 7 to 8 stitches per inch if by machine. There is no wrong or right way to stitch. Just make sure you take even stitches and anchor both the beginning and end of the seam with a knot, stitching backward for a few stitches, or staystitching in one place for a few stitches. Stitch from the beginning to the end of the top piece, through all three layers.

Step Two: Fold the second scrap back so the stitched seam is underneath the pieces and both pieces' front sides are now facing up. Press flat with an iron. (Use medium heat and a pressing cloth for fancy fabrics.) Then trim off any extra of the first fabric from the stitched seam, leaving about a 1/2" for a seam allowance.

Step Four, in fabric.

> **Tip:** You can hand-press a scrap or two by scraping your fingernail along the finished seam, but it's wise to keep an iron nearby for quick pressing after every third seam or so.

Step Three: Add a third scrap piece on top of your already-pieced section, placing your new fabric wrong side up, so all fabrics are front sides together. Stitch in place as you did the second piece.

Step Four: Press the newest piece back in place, then trim off extra fabric again.

Step Five: Continue these steps, adding not only fabrics, but also trims, until your background fabric is covered with Crazy patchwork. You're going to cut this block to size (or "square it up"—meaning trim it against a square ruler). So stitch right to the edge of the background fabric.

You'll want to experiment with laying trim so it either angles across previous fabric pieces or edges the fabric scrap you're currently adding. (The Victorians often added wide, flat silk or grosgrain ribbons, as well as fabrics.) If you come to a spot where your next patch can't fit the area needed, try appliquéing a fabric patch or piece of ribbon on top, or experiment with a Montano patch. (See sidebar on page 107.)

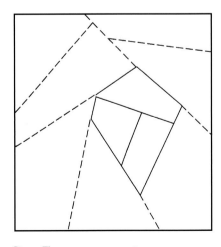

Step Five: *Continue stitching, pressing back, and trimming until the block is done! Square-up block edges.*

Tip: Fold a piece of lace or trim and insert it on top of the previous patch's edge, so the folded edges "fouff" out and the raw edges match the underneath patch's raw edges. Pin the fouff, then layer and stitch your next fabric patch in place. Result? A fluffy three-dimensional puff on your work! This works especially well for bits and pieces of handkerchiefs and netting.

Fouff (pronounced "foof"), two versions. You'll want to experiment with lace, bridal illusion, and other lightweight fabrics.

Step Six: Once you've filled your background foundation with Crazy patchwork to the edges, press it and quickly baste around the edge by hand or machine. Add embroidery, embellishments, or other decorations, but leave the outer 1" free of decoration, for stitching ease when you edge or join the block units. If you're doing a smaller quilt, you may want to leave off embroidering and embellishing until the blocks are joined and any borders or sashing are added. For a larger quilt, see below. If making a larger-size quilt, stitch as many blocks as needed to finish the quilt.

Basic Crazy foundation block, stitched and with embellishment beginning. Now's the time to start adding embroidery by machine or hand, as well.

Tip: If you will be piecing together several Crazy blocks to make a larger-size quilt top, embroider and embellish as you go and leave the outer 1" edge of the block free, as directed above. But wait to add bumpy things like buttons, charms, or beading until the blocks are joined. Your joined pieces will be more smooth and even.

Tip: If making multiple units that will be joined together, use a rotary cutter, ruler, and mat to trim each unit to the size you decided on (finished dimensions, plus $\frac{1}{2}$" seam allowance all around). A rectangular ruler works nicely, but a square ruler helps you see the look of the finished block through the plastic as you trim. Taking a few minutes to carefully trim gives you much nicer, smoother results when the pieces are joined. Remember the carpenter's rule: measure twice, cut once.

When using the stitch-and-flip method described in the Basic Crazy method, it's not unusual to sew your way into a dilemma. At some point, you run into an odd shape or area and can't continue, because you can't figure out how to cover it. The way out is a simple one: the Montano Patch. Although I've noticed this method used in much older quilts, Judith Baker Montano, one of Crazy quilting's best-known authors, made it famous.

Here's all you need to do: stitch two or more scraps together without stitching them to the background fabric (see diagram). Treat this pieced section as if it were one fabric scrap, fit it into your problem area, and continue merrily piecing on your way.

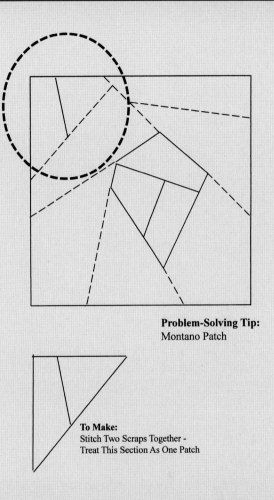

Problem-Solving Tip:
Montano Patch

To Make:
Stitch Two Scraps Together -
Treat This Section As One Patch

ABOVE: *Sew together two patches of any size and shape for this helpful "fix."*

The Montano Patch, popularized by Judith Baker Montano, provides an easy way to solve Crazy piecing problems. To make, stitch two scraps together and treat this section as one patch.

LEFT: *This Basic Crazy block shows a Montano patch in action—look at the top center, just above the photo-transfer of the girl with the fan. (Hint: The fabrics are the same as the patch example shown.)*

"Shady Ladies" | Date: 1998 | Maker: Cindy Brick | Size: 18" x 17 $\frac{1}{2}$ "

Basic Crazy method, finished project. This hand-stitched Crazy began as an exercise in shading, but I challenged myself to use as many different textiles as possible, including Grandma's damask napkin, a 1960s brocade skirt, and Daughter's Peter Pan blouse collar. Real actress cigarette silks (now sadly shredding—I used photo transfers after this) peer from behind the lacy "balconies." Actresses had a rather shady reputation at the turn of the century . . . thus the name. (Collection of the author. Photograph by Mellisa Karlin Mahoney.)

"Brick Family Crazy" | Date: 1999 | Maker: Cindy Brick | Size: 28 $\frac{1}{2}$" x 23 $\frac{1}{2}$"

Basic Crazy method, finished project. This machine- and hand-stitched Strippy-style quilt sandwiches three 6" x 17" panels between two 2"-wide strips, then encloses them all with a 3 $\frac{1}{4}$"-wide border. (All measurements finished size.) Various parts of the Brick family's saga are documented here, including our daughters Jess (the pigtailed blond in upper right, now a mature 21) and Angel (the huntress in bottom left, now 19). Embellishments include photo transfers, pins, cigarette silks, an antique cat head charm, ribbon roses . . . and a found orphan earring. (Collection of Jessica Brick. Photograph by Mellisa Karlin Mahoney.)

Paper Foundation Piecing (Easy Ways), basic block. This is the finished block, but wait to add embroidery and embellishments until the top is completed. (Don't remove the paper until the blocks are joined.)

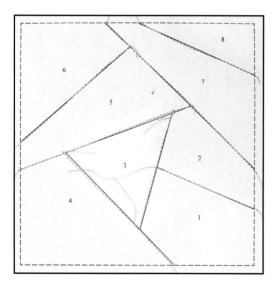

This method has an unusual approach—you stitch on the block's paper-pattern back, with the fabrics that make up the block underneath! Strange. But with practice, you'll find this accurate method very rewarding.

2. Paper Foundation Piecing (Easy Ways)

In paper foundation piecing, you position your fabric scraps underneath a paper pattern, then sew the scraps in place by stitching along the lines marked on the paper's top. If you prefer that all your finished units have an even, geometric look, this is the method for you. It is the most accurate technique for reproducing the same Crazy block over and over, and it can be done by hand or using a sewing machine.

A variation is String piecing, in which your background foundation is cut from newspaper or fabric. Then strings, or thin strips of various fabric scraps, are stitched diagonally on it, using the stitch-and-flip method described above. In this method, the fabrics are stitched *on top* of the foundation. In paper foundation piecing, they're stitched *underneath* the foundation. (English paper piecing, though it sounds similar, is actually quite different. See page 33 for more on this method.)

The paper foundation piecing instructions given here will have you piecing your Crazy on paper. Don't worry about the paper damaging your patchwork—it is removed when the top is finished. If you prefer a cloth background foundation, you can trace the block pattern given onto fabric. This method can be done by hand or machine, but is much faster by machine.

If you have never tried paper foundation piecing before, you'll find books by Carol Doak invaluable. *Quiltmaker* magazine also regularly runs step-by-step instructions for this method.

Materials

- The items for method one (Basic Crazy piecing), with the exception of the fabric background, unless you intend to trace the blocks onto fabric. Note: This method does not use heavily napped fabrics as effectively as method one. Try stitching your study block with cottons until you get the basic hang of it.
- Black-and-white photocopies of the block pattern on page 111: one copy per block, plus three or four extras, just in case. Note: You can use a photocopy of the pattern in the book, but label it "master" and use only it for each of the succeeding copies. The pattern provided is 6" finished. If you'd prefer a different size, just enlarge or reduce it on the photocopier, but still make sure to label your revised pattern "master" and use it to make additional photocopies.

Directions

Step One: Trim each photocopy so that there is approximately $\frac{1}{2}$" of paper left *outside* the outermost solid line. Select a fabric scrap roughly the size of block section #1, but extending at least $\frac{1}{2}$" outside the marked lines of #1. Fit the patch *underneath* the paper so it shadows #1. (Check by lifting the block up to a light source, such as a lamp or windowpane.) Pin in place, right side out.

Step Two: Choose a fabric scrap roughly the size of block section #2, plus about $\frac{1}{2}$" all around. (Position the fabric underneath the paper on patch #2 to check.) Turn the patch #2 fabric so it fits against patch #1—right sides

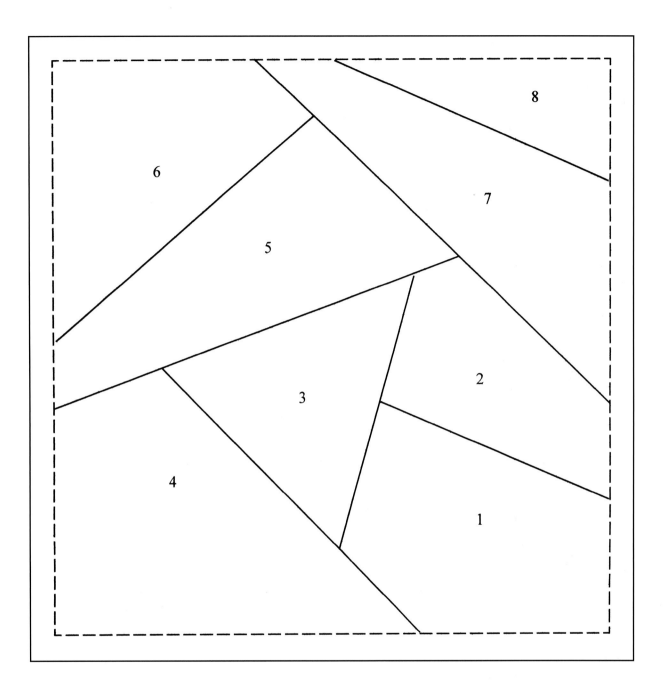

Paper Foundation Piecing (Easy Ways) pattern, actual 6" finished size. Use this block as your master photocopy pattern. It can be increased or decreased in size as needed, but use the same original pattern for each photocopy.

Block "front" with the stitched-paper "back" (actually the true front, while you're stitching) showing. Remember: With this method, you stitch on the paper backing with the fabrics positioned underneath!

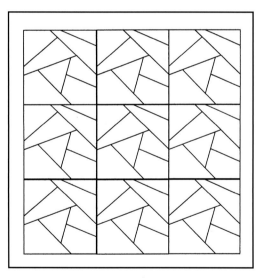

Paper Foundation Piecing (Easy Ways) nine-block quilt diagram, with border. Problem-solving tip: Flip the blocks in different directions to give a more random look.

together, "kissing each other." Pin or just hold in place. Stitch directly on the marked line that separates patches #1 and #2, using small, even stitching (10 to 12 per inch, if using a machine). (You actually use more stitches per inch with this method.) Trim the seam allowances by the stitched line to approximately ¹/₂", then flip patch #2 back. Press flat.

Step Three: Continue adding patches, following the numbers. For even more interest, add a length of flat trim or ribbon now and then along with the fabrics, or try layering more than two fabrics as you sew. See method one for ideas.

Step Four: Press the block, then trim it to size, using a rotary cutter, ruler, and mat, and the *marked solid outer line* as your cutting line. (The inner dashed line is used when stitching the blocks together.)

If constructing a multiblock quilt, use the method above to stitch as many blocks as needed. Vary fabrics and trims with each block. For the quilt diagram shown, you'll need nine paper foundation–pieced blocks. If you like the border shown, you'll also need approximately ¹/₂ yard of fabric to cut two 2¹/₂" border strips across the width of the fabric. Then cut these each in half for 4 border strips. This diagram would make a quilt 18" x 18" without borders or 22" x 22" with 2" finished borders.

To assemble your blocks into a quilt, continue with the following steps.

Step Five: Lay out your blocks in a three-by-three set. (Flip each block one half-turn for a less matchy-matchy look.) Stitch the blocks together, matching and using the dashed lines as a sewing guide. Press, then join rows together. If including borders, add one each on the sides, then on the top and bottom.

Step Six: Each of the paper patterns in your joined blocks should now be thoroughly perforated with stitching holes, kind of like multiple dotted lines! Use these perforations to gently fold and tear away the paper, using tweezers when needed to pull away some particularly stubborn bit.

> **Tip:** Tear away the paper only when your top is finished—before adding batting, backing, and binding. That way, each of the paper-foundation–pieced blocks are smoothly enclosed and not as apt to loosen or wear. You might even want to quickly baste around the top's edge if you're not planning to add borders. Follow the general directions to finish your quilt.

What if the fabric patch I used is too small, and the section didn't get covered, after all?

This is a simple fix: just position and stitch on another scrap of fabric until it is. Use the same fabric if you want the fix to blend in or a contrasting one if it's not important to have all the blocks exactly the same. If you're a little nervous about this, mark a new stitching line right on top of the paper, then stitch on that line to add the newest fabric patch. Trim away the extra, press it back, and continue on to the next marked section.

Oh no! I cut on the inner dashed line, instead of the outer solid line, when trimming the block!

No worries here, either—Crazy patchwork is remarkably forgiving. It just means that your finished block will be approximately ½" smaller all around, and your finished quilt will be correspondingly smaller.

Can I design my own Crazy-patched paper foundation–pieced block?

Yes, and easily! Just keep in mind that each section in your block must be covered on one side by the section stitched after it. (In the pattern given here, for example, section #1 is covered by #2. Both are covered by #3. Then section #4 covers #3 and a sliver of #1.) Straight lines must be used, but that doesn't mean they can't be short or angled. Just remember to cover each patch with the succeeding patch, and you'll be fine.

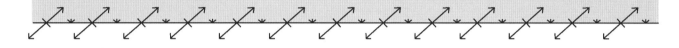

"Easy Ways" Nine-Block Crazy | Date: 2007 | Maker: Cindy Brick | Size: 22" x 22"

Paper foundation piecing makes this piece extra fast; you'll need nine photocopies of the pattern given. Move each block a quarter-turn while laying out the blocks, to give each a different look; use the quilt diagram on page 112 for help. Add a 2" border all around (2½" cut border strips) to finish. (Collection of the author. Photograph by Mellisa Karlin Mahoney.)

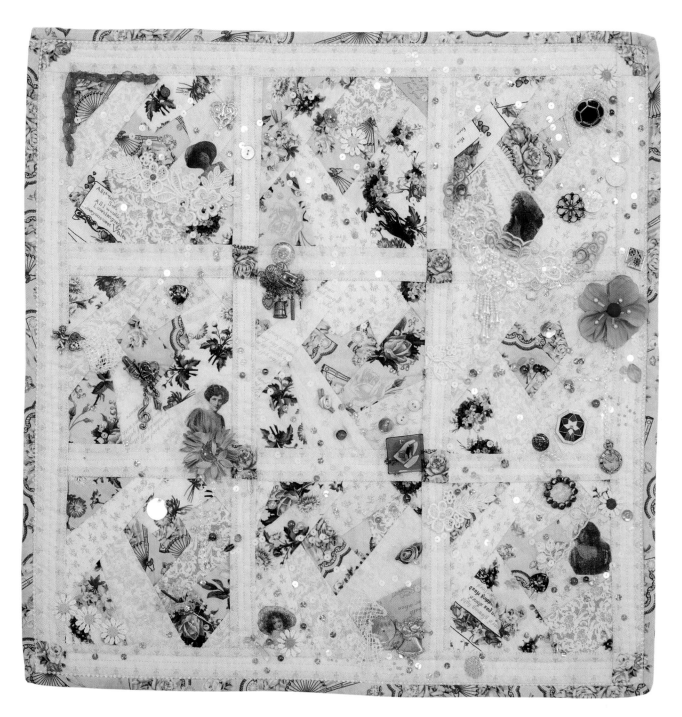

"Here's My Heart: A Language of Love Crazy Sampler" | Date: 2002 | Maker: Cindy Brick | Size: 24" x 24"
Fabrics from the author's "Language of Love" collection with Marcus Brothers were used to make this piece. Paper foundation piecing makes the "heart" shapes stand out. (Collection of the author. Photograph by Mellisa Karlin Mahoney.)

3. Shadow Crazy Piecing (Light-Speed Crazy)

Of the three Crazy piecing methods given, this one is by far the fastest. It was originally inspired by a quilted wearable technique by Bird Ross, by Shelly Burge's "confetti" method, by a 1980s technique called shadow quilting, and by some modern art quilts. But the combination is my own. This method is primarily for the sewing machine, though hand stitching can also be used.

Materials

- The items mentioned in method one. Note: Although heavily napped fabrics can be used, you'll get better results without them. Sequins are an exciting touch, especially hologram or iridescent styles.
- Netting (the smaller the holes, the better), tulle, or another sheer fabric approximately 2" larger than the foundation fabric. (If you're making more than one unit, you'll need one piece of netting per unit.)
- A can of spray photo adhesive (the acid-free kind used to attach photos in scrapbooks).
- Decorative thread for machine stitching. (Metallics, hologram, or any textured threads work nicely.)

Directions

Follow the directions given in method one to cut your foundation fabric unit(s).

Step One: Lay the foundation unit on a flat surface and smooth in place. Quickly (and lightly!) spray its surface with photo adhesive. You'll have about a half-hour to work before the tacky surface doesn't adhere any more. Cut and randomly lay fabric scraps down on the surface of the fabric, letting them overlap occasionally. Remember: The bigger the scrap, the more quickly your foundation will be covered. Feel free to add photo transfers, specially cut motifs from fabric prints, lace, trim, and other flat embellishments as you go. But leave off any embellishments that protrude from the surface, like buttons.

Step Two: Continue to lay fabric patches down, overlapping as you go, until the fabric background is covered, right to the edge.

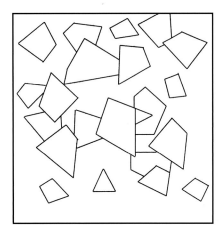

Step One: *Randomly lay patches on prepared background square.*

> **Tip:** Use a patterned or textured print or specialty woven fabric (such as a white-on-white cotton print or a satin) for the background fabric unit. Add sheer netting or lace in some spots for a peek-a-boo effect.

Step Three: Center the netting or sheer fabric piece over the unit and gently press it down to cover the scraps and give the Crazy patchwork a cloudy effect.

Step Four: Now comes the fun part! Using decorative machine thread, randomly stitch all over your quilt top, swirling and turning as you go. Take care to stitch at least once through every fabric patch. This is a good time to try those decorative stitches you've been meaning to experiment with, but a straight or zigzag stitch works just fine, too. Stitch until you're

Step One beginning, in fabric.

happy with the looks of your block. Variation: Instead of random stitching, outline every fabric patch on the block for a more traditional look. This is another good way to experiment with your machine's decorative stitches; hand embroidery works well, too.

> **Tip:** Try switching threads occasionally to give a richer surface look. If you're having trouble with the heavier machine threads catching and breaking in the needle, try threading your bobbin with them instead. Use regular thread in the top needle. Then turn the quilt top over and stitch randomly, back side up.

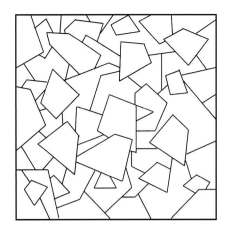

Step Two: *Continue adding patches until block is covered.*

Step Five: If making more than one unit, stitch as many as needed. Add embroidery or embellishments, as desired, then trim to your desired size. (See method one.) Follow the general directions to finish your quilt.

> **Tip:** If making multiple blocks, randomly stitch each one as it's finished, trim to size, then join the blocks to make your quilt top. Or make the blocks, trim each to size, join, then start the decorative stitching for a more consistent look overall. Either way works.

Step Two, in fabric.

JOINING YOUR CRAZY PATCHWORK UNITS

Regardless of the piecing method used, if you've made multiple Crazy-patched blocks, you'll need to join them. Lay the blocks out in rows in the block set you prefer. Now is the time to cut and add sashing strips to the laid-out blocks, if you're going to use them. Use a ¼" seam and stitch by hand or machine. Work slowly for best results, keeping your seams as even as possible.

> **Tip:** For best results, take a minute to mark a stitching line on the back of each block, drawing the line ¼" inside from the unit edge. Match and pin blocks, taking care to make sure your pins go through both blocks' marked lines. Stitch directly on the marked line.

Step Three, in fabric.

Join the blocks (and sashing units, if used) row by row, pressing with an iron as you finish each seam, first from the back, then from the front. Use a pressing cloth to minimize damaging fancy fabrics. Join the finished rows, then press the completed quilt top.

If you plan to use a border, add it now—sides first, then top and bottom. (Consult a general quiltmaking book for more information on cutting and sewing on borders.) Press the quilt top one more time.

If you like, now take some time to add bulky embellishments and embroider the joining seams of the units. You can also do this after the quilt is finished.

This example of the Shadow Crazy method is embellished with embroidery, sequins, and buttons. (Pieced, machine embroidered, and finished by Mary Waller and Cindy Brick.)

This Shadow Crazy block-in-progress features a central photo transfer of Arthur and Rena DeVries and their children. (Pieced by Art and Rena's granddaughter, Cindy [DeVries] Brick.)

"Our House Is a Very, Very, Very Fine House," Study #1 | Date: 2005 | Maker: Cindy Brick | Size: 16" x 16"
This quilt features a paper foundation–pieced house center with a Light-Speed Crazy border. It was machine- and hand-pieced and machine embroidered using the Road Warrior technique (page 131). (Collection of the author. Photograph by Mellisa Karlin Mahoney.)

"Our House Is a Very, Very, Very Fine House," Study #2 | Date: 2005 | Maker: Cindy Brick | Size: 18" x 18"
See how different the same technique can seem when using different fabrics? Instead of netting, both of these borders use multiple lines of random machine stitching to keep the patches in place. (Collection of the author. Photograph by Mellisa Karlin Mahoney.)

FINISHING YOUR CRAZY

Cut a backing fabric at least 4" larger all around than your top. If making a large-size quilt, you may have to piece together two or three widths of fabric to get the size you need.

You'll also need a piece of cotton batting, preferably bonded, in the same size as the backing. Get the thinnest batting available or split a thicker one in half. Your quilt will be heavy enough without the extra weight.

Spread out your backing fabric and smooth it, then add the batting and finally the quilt top to make a textile sandwich. (Think of the batting as the meat and the backing and top as bread slices.) Baste your quilt, using sewing thread and the longest needle possible.

Tie or Quilt?

Tying

Because of their bulk, traditional Crazies were almost always tied or tacked. To keep your quilt visually clean, try tacking from the top or tying the quilt on the back, instead of the front. Here's how to do it.

For a larger quilt, gently roll it up on both ends until you have approximately a 36- to 48-inch working area in the quilt center. Secure the rolled ends with bicycle clips or ribbon ties, then lay the quilt out on a large table. For a smaller quilt, just lay it flat on the table. You can also use a quilt frame or hoop to hold the working area steady, but keep the pressure on the quilt top to a minimum. Too much pressure will damage your embroidery and fabrics.

Work from the top of the quilt, using a long needle and strong thread. (Silk thread is excellent, but cotton will do.) Slide one hand underneath the working area. At each block join, stitch down through all three layers until your bottom hand feels the needle. Gently maneuver the needle back up to the top of the quilt, through all three layers, to the same spot on top where you stitched. Repeat this two to three times to tack the quilt in place. Then run your needle just underneath the quilt top's surface to the next tacking spot and repeat the procedure.

Twentieth-century Crazy quilters frequently used yarn for tying their quilts—and you can, too. But yarn ties give an odd, unshaven look to the top, so tie them on the back or underneath side, instead. Begin your tying from the underneath side of the quilt, using the basic method. Tie with long pieces of yarn, leaving tails of yarn at the beginning and the end. When you finish, tie each pair of yarn tails into a pretty bow, then trim all ends to the same size. Ribbon bows or yarn pompons can also be stitched to each tacked/tied spot for a dainty look.

Tack or tie at each corner of each unit, or approximately every 6 to 12 inches. Keep your quilt layers as smooth and even as possible as you go. Work from the center outward.

Quilting

If you machine or hand quilt your piece, use the same general layering and basting methods, but keep your quilting to a minimum. I'd recommend outline quilting the blocks and border edges, but save your time and energy for quilting other patchwork styles. After all, it's the embroidery and embellishments that take center stage in a Crazy. If you've decided to add a border to your quilt, that area is excellent for quilting a motif or special designs.

Binding

Use a general quiltmaking book to help you cut binding strips and bind your Crazy. For any size quilt, I usually figure on 1 yard of firm-woven silk or polished cotton, cut in $2\frac{1}{2}$-inch-long strips the width of fabric, then pressed in half lengthwise for a French binding. This doubled binding is easier to stitch on accurately and wears better than a single-layer binding. (You may need 2 yards of fabric, cut in $2\frac{1}{2}$-inch-wide strips, for an extra-large, queen- or king-sized quilt.)

Note: Silk has a definite grain that will affect your stitching. Make stitching silk easier by cutting enough binding strips from the *width* of the fabric; join them to make binding strips for the length of two sides of the quilt. Then cut enough binding strips from the *length* of the silk for the quilt top and bottom; join and stitch in place. Fold the binding at each corner, then trim extra away from the foldline.

I'm timid about color combinations. How do I choose the right ones?

One way to ensure success is to stick to one or two color families when choosing the majority of your fabrics. (You can add one or two other colors as accents.) For lots of bright contrast, choose colors that are directly opposite each other on the color wheel, like red and blue. For a more blended look, choose colors that are next to each other on the color wheel: blue and green, blue and purple, pink and yellow, for example.

My quilt looks a little boring. What did I do wrong?

You probably fell into the Crazy quilter's greatest downfall: using just solid colors or trying too hard to match everything. Overmatching is the bane of any quilt style. You'll have a much more interesting piece if you mix solids, textures, and prints. You'll want a range of small, medium, and large scraps, too. Choose a print that includes your favorite colors, then build off it. Or try a variety of textures; instead of just plain velvet, for example, include embossed or burned-out floral versions, too. Don't be afraid to mix fibers—marbled cottons look amazing next to Chinese woven silks!

If your background section is already pieced, don't despair—see the next question. And you can always add embellishments to perk up a sedate color scheme!

What if I finish a unit and find that one of the fabrics or trims is clashing with the rest of the block?

If you can't remove the item in question, try stitching another fabric, piece of lace, or large embellishment on top. (This works well for other quilt tops and even finished projects, too, as long as you take care to stitch only through the top layer.) Doilies and lace medallions are especially good for cover-up work. So are groups of buttons and beads. You may find this camouflaged area turns out to be your favorite part!

Do I add trims while I'm piecing the Crazy unit or afterwards?

You can do both. I like to add flatter items while piecing, then the heavier, more textured items later, after the block is finished and I'm embellishing. Try leaving an open area, approximately $1/2$ inch, here and there while you're piecing. Later, you can slide lace or other trims into these open areas and stitch in place.

The heavier nap on some fabrics, like velvet, is a real hassle to stitch. How can I make it easier?

Try what the Victorians did—stitch right on the plain-woven selvage, instead of struggling to fold or turn under the velvet nap. That way, you won't be dealing with the thicker bulk of the folded edge. Victorian-era quilters would baste the selvage down, then embroider on top of it or cover the selvage with ribbon. (Grosgrain was a favorite of theirs, but you can use all different types).

Hand piecing is the only right way to stitch a traditional-style Crazy, right?

Nope. Even the Crazy's earliest makers, during a time when handwork was encouraged, occasionally stitched their blocks by machine (mostly after 1850, when the sewing machine had become generally available in America, that is). Today's quilters use a variety of hand and machine techniques—often in the same quilt. Many Crazies are machine pieced and joined, then hand embroidered and embellished. Whatever you choose to do, try to make your work as even and thought-out as possible. Take your time, and do it right.

What happens if I make a mistake?

Here's the great wonder of Crazy quiltmaking—you can't! At least you can't make any mistake that can't be covered up or added to. (Some Crazy quilters never technically finish a piece—years later, they're still adding a ribbon rose here, a beaded detail there.) Many a glorious Crazy quilt detail has resulted from someone's goof. Think of the freedom this gives you to experiment and try different techniques!

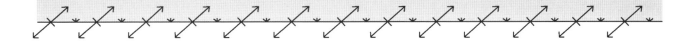

Velvet and Satin Crazy | Date: ca. 1885–1895 | Maker: Unknown, probably Minnesota | Size: 53¾" x 62"

The wide lace edging of this piece was a popular way to show off expensive and/or handmade lace. Few lace edgings have survived on antique Crazies; usually they wore out decades ago and were discarded. The political ribbons are of Grover Cleveland (who ran successfully for President in 1884 and 1892—but lost in 1888) and Edmund Rice, once mayor of Saint Paul, Minnesota, and a U.S. congressman at his death in 1889. (Minnesota Historical Society)

These key embroidery stitches are taken, with kind permission, from Dorothy Bond's classic *Crazy Quilt Stitches*. (See the additional resources list for specifics on this fine handbook.)

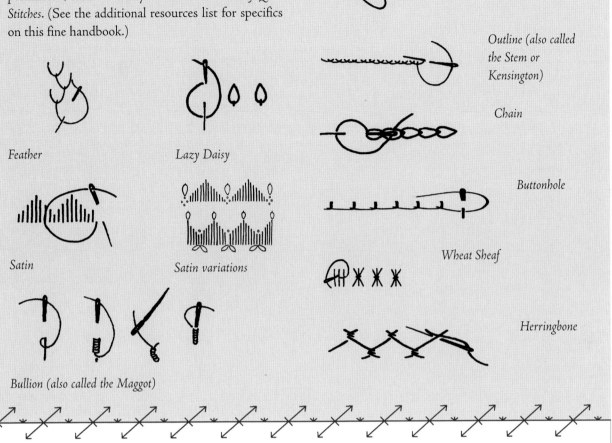

Running

Outline (also called the Stem or Kensington)

Chain

Feather

Lazy Daisy

Buttonhole

Satin

Satin variations

Wheat Sheaf

Herringbone

Bullion (also called the Maggot)

Stitch in place. In effect, you're using the vertical fabric grain for two sides of the quilt and the horizontal grain for the top and bottom. I can't give you a technical reason for why this works—I can only say that from hard experience, it does.

Another traditional method is the edges-turned-together method. Trim the quilt top, batting, and backing edges to the same size. Now turn the top edge under approximately ½ inch; do the same with the backing fabric, and fit the folded edges together, pushing back the batting slightly as you go. Pin or just hold the folded edges together with your fingers, and hand whipstitch or machine topstitch in place. Victorian Crazy quilters would often (but not always) add fringe to this quilt edge; a wide border of knitted, tatted, or crocheted lace; or a stitched-on edging of gimp. (We know this glossy, twisted cording better from its use in home decorating, where it's used for edging pillows or tying back curtains.) Sometimes more embroidery was added along the edge as a finish instead.

Why don't we see gimp, lace, or fringe more often on old Crazy quilts? The answer is simple: it was removed. When a Crazy quilt's edges were turned and whipstitched together, they often wore out faster than if they'd been bound with a separate binding. An easy way to camouflage this damage was to remove the edging, which had taken most of the wear. And that is exactly what happened in most cases. (To tell for sure, look for needle marks and uneven wear patterns.) This is especially evident on Victorian silk Crazy quilts. Sometimes the quilt was cut down slightly and rebound with a separate binding instead.

This method's tendency to wear out quickly is why it is not as popular today for newly made Crazies.

"Hearts and Flowers" | Date: 1996 | Maker: Christine Dabbs | Size: 44" x 54"

Christine Dabbs of Costa Mesa, California, took approximately eight months to hand-stitch this piece, including silk threadwork and beading. (She doesn't even own a sewing machine!) Most of the motifs and border designs were inspired by or adapted from Helen Stevens' books The Embroiderer's Country Album *and* The Embroiderer's Countryside. *The quilt took first place at the International Quilt Association (IQA) show in 1996, as well as first place and a Viewers Choice award at Road to California two years later.*

Chris designed and stitched all of the Crazy quilts used as part of the movie How to Make an American Quilt. *She is also the author of a book on Crazies, featuring her special stitching methods. (Collection of the quiltmaker. Photograph by Mellisa Karlin Mahoney.)*

EMBROIDERING AND EMBELLISHING YOUR CRAZY QUILT

Crazies today lend themselves to a wide variety of surface techniques, including machine and hand embroidery; beading; charms, buttons, and other three-dimensional additions; even stamping and hand painting. You'll want to try a little of each one.

Embroidery: By Hand or Machine

Victorian-era Crazy quilts are rich in embroidery of every possible kind and description. Generally, every single patch in a nineteenth-century Crazy was outlined in some kind of stitchwork; the only exceptions are the very early cotton Crazies, which were rarely ornamented or were done using just one kind of stitch. Depression-era cotton Crazy patches were often outlined with black buttonhole or feather stitches, using cotton floss.

Embroidering by Hand

The Victorians admired fine hand stitching, and there seems to have been an ongoing competition to load each Crazy patch with one, two, or three different stitch combinations. The same four stitches predominate, though: the outline or Kensington stitch, the stem, the feather, and the herringbone. A combination of different colors was often used, too, though the thread material was generally the same: silk floss. (They called it art silk or thread painting silk.)

Today's silk floss is not generally as brightly colored or as heavy as nineteenth-century floss. But there is a happy substitute: rayon floss, which comes in a wide palette of color and reflects light in much the same way as its predecessor. Like cotton floss, each "rope" can be separated into six strands; use two together when embroidering your Crazy quilt. Embroidery needles are easiest to use, but I'm partial to the new wide-eyed quilting betweens, as well.

The stitch diagrams provided in the accompanying sidebar should be of help to you for adding embroidery to your Crazy quilt. Try practicing on a scrap piece of fabric until you've got the basic stitch down, then begin with an inconspicuous area on your Crazy. Use your newly learned stitch to outline the

This nineteenth-century skein of "art silk" (silk embroidery floss for Crazy quilting) is heavier and glossier than our silk floss today.

patch, then move on to another patch on the opposite side of the quilt. (You can always come back and add more to the first section.) Experiment with combining stitches, stitching one set, then adding others on top as you follow around each scrap. Beads are a beautiful addition to embroidery and are added last of all.

Embroidering by Machine

Many of today's sewing machines have a variety of decorative stitches—now's the time to try them out. This is actually a long-standing tradition; sewing machine trade cards showing a variety of stitches and embroidery patterns were popular in the 1880s and after. Your sewing machine's instruction book should

Continued on page 130

Victorian Crazy | Date: 1886 | Maker: Unknown, possibly Illinois | Size: 57" x 61"
This remarkable Crazy holds a number of beautifully painted motifs and is stitched from "fancies," the elaborate fabrics of the day, including "voided" velvets. At one point, it was registered with the Illinois State Quilt Project (No. LA-116). (Collection of Maury Bynum. Photograph by Mellisa Karlin Mahoney.)

"Olde Fashion Romance" | Date: 2001 | Maker: Nancy Eha | Size: 25" x 21"

Nancy Eha, of Stillwater, Minnesota, is known especially for her innovative beadwork. Beading is the primary design element in this hand-stitched piece, with hand embroidery and silk-ribbon embroidery taking a close second. (Photograph courtesy of the quiltmaker)

A boy and his umbrella are embroidered on this Crazy quilt square, circa 1890. (Collection of the author. Photograph by Teressa Mahoney, Forever Yours Photography.)

Continued from page 127

guide you in the specifics. Try using these stitches to outline stitch each scrap, switching decorative threads occasionally.

> **Tip:** Using an ombre decorative thread lets you switch colors automatically as you stitch! Choose a bright-colored shade that will contrast with your quilt's fabrics for best effect.

Embroidered Motifs

Many an old Crazy quilt features one or more beautifully stitched images. (See "Popular Crazy Themes" in part one for more on these.) Sometimes the motifs are outline stitched, using one color (and two threads) of floss. Sometimes they're much more substantial; these filled-in motifs are generally stitched with silk floss (chenille was also used on occasion) in a technique the Victorians called thread painting. We know it today as satin stitch, and it's done with a variety of colors, carefully blended.

You can try stitching your own motifs using the antique patterns provided in the appendix on page 134. (Check one of the Crazy quilt books mentioned in the additional resources section for more instructions and help.) Some quilters enjoy marking and stitching motifs on a fabric scrap, then piecing the embroidered patch into their Crazy top. Others prefer to trace and add their motifs in the larger fabric patches on a finished Crazy top. You might try both ways to see which you like best.

> **Tip:** To trace patterns onto a piece of fabric, lay the pattern, then the fabric on a light table or sunlit window. The bright background light allows the pattern to show through the fabric clearly.

> **Tip:** Try marking your motifs with a water-erasable blue marking pen; the marks are easy to sponge away when the embroidery is done. Or if the fabric in question is not washable, try the traditional tool: a freshly sharpened pencil.

> **Tip:** Most stitchers and quilters feel comfortable enough outlining the fabric patches with embroidery—it's the motifs that frighten them. If you feel uneasy about your embroidery skills, you might take advantage of the modern version of the purchased Victorian-era embroideries: iron-on appliqué patches. These are available in a wide variety of subjects and styles and come ready to be ironed and/or stitched in place. They're surprisingly similar to the machine-stitched embroidery motifs offered for sale during the Victorian period. The only thing that will tell others you've used these ready-made appliqués are their raised edges or the small whipstitches holding them in place. (See pages 47 and 48.)

This embellishment technique was inspired by the futuristic *Mad Max* movies, where bad guys ran their victims down with fantastic road vehicles—before, that is, they became roadkill themselves. The method is perfect for when you've had a horrible day. The dog just threw up, your income tax is due, and the washer just spewed water everywhere! Never mind. It will be better soon.

Piece and cover a quilt top, using any of the methods above. (The Shadow Crazy is my favorite for this method.) Thread your machine with decorative thread, preferably a metallic. You'll also need a yard of sequins (although terrible, horrible, no-good, very bad days might require more). Pull the sequins off their string in a group of five, seven, or nine, then scatter them randomly across the surface of your quilt.

Humming cheerfully, set off to chase down each sequin and run it over! (You can do this by hand too, but it's not quite as effective. Chuckle fiendishly, and your family may look strangely at you.) The sequins may be caught with your first line of stitching, but more often, they skitter and run in front of the presser foot. No matter. Just keep on until the last sequin has been tossed, caught, and *stitched*!

You'll end up with a nice random scribble design across the surface of your quilt, accented here and there with sparkling sequins. Try it—the Road Warrior method works wonders on your peace of mind. Kids like it, too—especially little boys. (See samples on pages 120 and 121.)

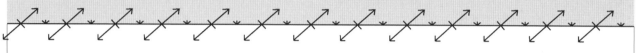

Painting

In Victorian times, the ability to paint realistically was useful not only for china and decorative pieces, but Crazy quilts, as well. Most of the time, painting was done with oil paints. Unfortunately, those same painted surfaces are cracking, dulling, and peeling today, thanks to the chemicals and minerals, especially iron, used in the original paints.

Painted laces and appliqués make beautiful accompaniments to Crazy quilting; they dress up photo transfers and plainer fabrics and trims, too.

You may enjoy experimenting with oils or acrylics on fabric. Or try the following simple hand-painting technique, which works on lace and trims. I came up with this method after doing research in antique periodicals, watching a class by Judith Baker Montano (who used watercolors to paint her homemade fabric transfers), and admiring (expensive) hand-dyed lace pieces that did not fit in my budget. (For an expansion and step-by-step description of this method, visit my 2008 book *Hanky Panky with a Flourish*.)

In short, you can paint fabric, lace, and even ribbon with any watercolor paints—as long as you heat-set the still-wet surface until the item is dry. This is most easily done with a hot iron and a scrap of muslin large enough to fold in half. Put the wet item on top of the muslin and fold in half again to cover. (This folded muslin will absorb any paint that bleeds off as you heat-set.) Press the folded muslin sandwich until the painted item is dry. You can repeat this process as much as you like, as long as you heat-set before painting again. The painted surface can be any look you want, and best of all, it's generally colorfast. (If you don't believe me, test a painted piece. It may leak a bit of color in the first wash, but will stay colorfast after that, provided you heat-set it while the watercolor paint was still wet.)

Beads, Buttons, and Other Three-Dimensional Embellishments

Any Crazy quilt would be improved with the addition of these lovely items; they add color and pattern—and hide mistakes, as well! Experiment with a variety of sizes and finishes, if you like, but if you're nervous about the total effect, stick with one or two color families. Whatever you choose, your quilt will be even more interesting if the embellishments not only reflect light, but also reflect more than one color. I am particularly fond of pearls and iridescent or hologram items. They're also budget helpers. One iridescent trim, for

The Brainerd & Armstrong Silk Company of Philadelphia, Pennsylvania, promotes their "wash silks" in this advertisement from the late 1800s.

example, will complement a wide variety of different colors and styles.

Silk thread is excellent for attaching these items. It's strong, supple, and visually disappears into the surface of the quilt. If you can't find silk, then choose the thinnest, strongest cotton or clear polyester thread. Silk is worth the search, though, and is readily available online, as well as in quilting and beading stores.

I tend to use embellishments two different ways: either I feature them, alone or in a small group, or I scatter them randomly across the surface of the quilt. (See the sidebar on the Road Warrior technique for my treatment of sequins.) Larger embellishments—especially items such as pins—benefit from being put in the spotlight. Your grandma's treasured cameo will look positively elegant in a space reserved especially for it. (If you attach these jewelry items separately, you can wear them, then replace them on the quilt when you're done.)

The possibilities are endless for embellishments. Just in case you need some ideas, though, here are some unusual sources:

- *From your dresser drawer*: orphan jewelry (especially the lone earring!); necklaces that are too large, bulky, or out of style (unstring them and use the beads); cufflinks; old coins (especially souvenirs); trinkets from your children's or ancestors' baby days; embroidered and decorative details from old clothing, including collars, yokes, and such; sections from old belts.
- *From your kitchen and office drawers*: pins, small metal items, wire (especially copper, coiled into circles), parts from worn-out kitchen utensils, small cookie cutters.
- *From your photo album*: souvenir postcards, old letters, photos, scribbled messages.

Paper items—photos, postcards, letters, and such—can be used directly on the quilt. Cut and stitch four strips of trim—one for each corner of the item—to hold it in place, like the tabs in an old-time photograph album. Or these items can be photo-transferred onto fabric and stitched in place. (Warning: You cannot photo-transfer any commercial photo or design without writing for permission first, unless it was published at least seventy-five years ago and is therefore past its copyright. This is just a general guideline—there are always exceptions [Mickey Mouse, for example]. Check with a legal source if you have any doubts.)

Most found items already have small holes that can be used for stitching them in place or have fabric edges to stitch down. If they don't, you can glue them to jewelry findings, like pins, fishhook earrings, or shank buttons, then stitch, pin, or hook in place.

You can do it. You can make a Crazy. May your quilt be full of beauty—and special memories for you and your family.

APPENDIX

EMBROIDERY MOTIFS

Add a touch of history to your Crazy or embroidery project with these antique motifs pulled from *Needle-Craft, Godey's Lady's Book, Peterson's Magazine*, and various nineteenth-century catalogs and needlework guides.

To use them, photocopy a page, then tape the photocopy to a window. Trace directly onto your fabric patch, leaving at least 1" extra all around for trimming and seam allowances. (A washable blue marker is especially good for tracing, though an extra-fine marker or mechanical pencil works well, too.) Another method: Trim the motif on your photocopied page, leaving approximately $\frac{1}{2}$" extra all around. Pin it directly to the fabric and stitch, using the marked lines as a guide. Gently pull away the paper when your stitching is done.

Stitching

Crazy quilters once used silk floss for embroidery, but our modern version is too light and not glossy enough; try rayon floss (two to three strands) instead.

For an old-fashioned redwork look, try two

strands of No. 498 DMC cotton embroidery floss (one strand for faces and delicate details), and use the outline stitch. (See the embroidery stitch diagrams on page 125.)

A variety of stitches were used for motifs, but the most popular practice was either to outline stitch in colored threads, redwork style, or to fill in the motif with satin stitch, using the outline stitch for definition and detail.

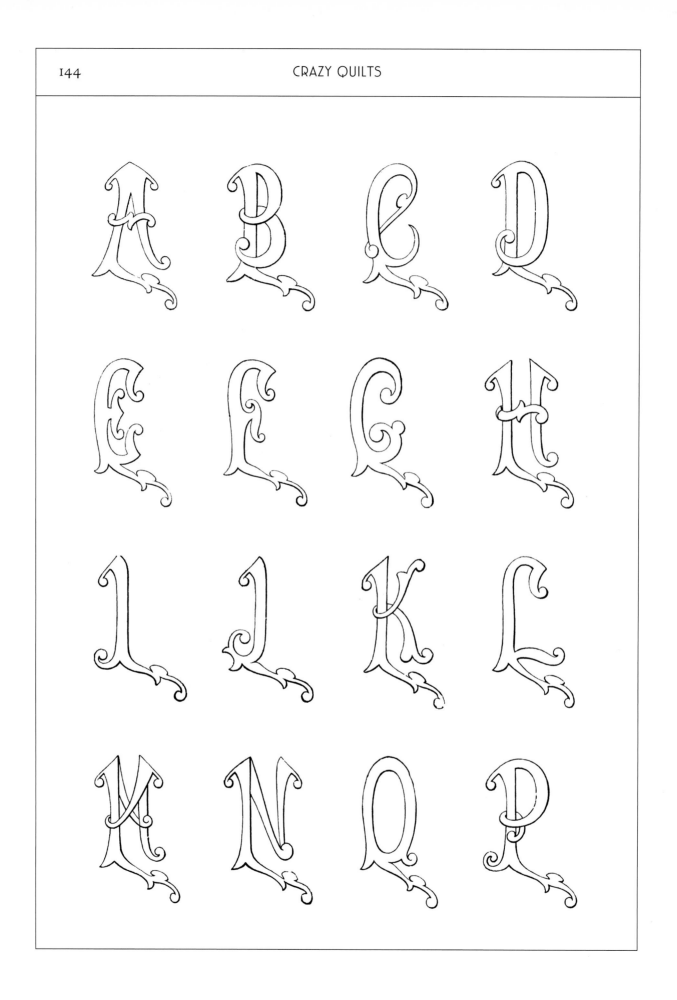

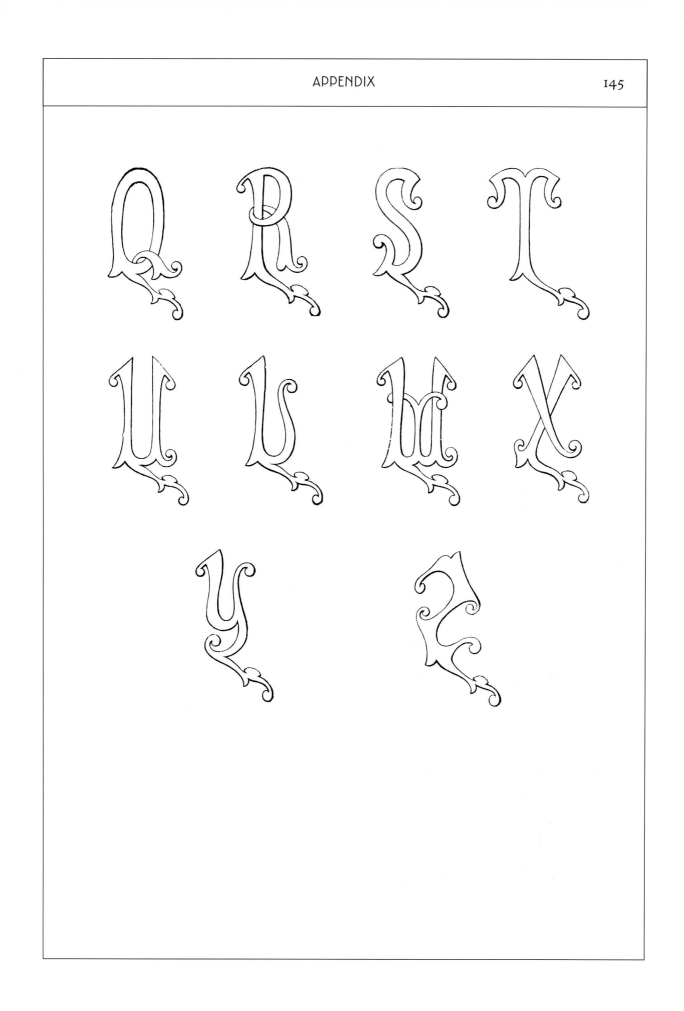

WORKS CITED

Alcott, Louisa M. "Patty's Patchwork," *Aunt Jo's Scrap-Bag*. Boston: Roberts Brothers, 1872.

Avery, Virginia. *Quilts to Wear*. New York: Dover Needlework, 1982.

Bassett, Lynne Z. and Jack Larkin. *Northern Comfort: New England's Early Quilts 1780-1850*. Nashville: Rutledge Hill Press, 1998.

Bishop, Robert. *New Discoveries in American Quilts*. New York: E. P. Dutton, 1975.

Bishop, Robert and Jacqueline M. Atkins. *Folk Art in American Life*. New York: Viking Studio Books, 1995.

Bowman, Doris. *American Quilts: The Smithsonian Treasury*. Washington, D.C.: Smithsonian Institution Press, 1991.

Brackman, Barbara. *Kansas Quilts & Quilters*. Lawrence: University Press of Kansas, 1993.

Clark, Ricky. "Ruth Finley and the Colonial Revival Era." In *Uncoverings 1995, Volume 16*. Edited by Virginia Gunn. Lincoln, NE: American Quilt Study Group, 1995.

Cognac, Camille Dalphond. *Quilt Restoration: A Practical Guide*. McClean, VA: EPM Publications, 1994.

Gunn, Virginia. "Quilts-Crazy Memories" In *America's Glorious Quilts*, edited by Dennis Duke and Deborah Harding. New York: Beaux Arts Editions/Hugh Lauter Levin Associates, 1987.

Colby, Averil. *Patchwork Quilts*. New York: Charles Scribner's Sons, 1965.

Crazy Patchwork: All the New Fancy Stitches Illustrated. Philadelphia: Strawbridge & Clothier, 1884. Excerpted in *Piecework*, March/April 1998.

Crowley, David. *An Introduction to the Victorian Style*. New York: Shooting Star Press, 1990.

Davis, Nancy. "The Kaleidoscope Quilt." In *Eyewinkers, Tumbleturds and Candlebugs: The Art of Elizabeth Talford Scott*. Baltimore: Maryland Institute College of Art, 1998. Published in conjunction with the exhibition "Eyewinkers, Tumbleturds and Candlebugs: The Art of Elizabeth Talford Scott" shown at the Maryland Institute College of Art in 1999.

Dorner, Jane. *Fashion: The Changing Shape of Fashion Through the Years*. London, WI: Octopus Books, 1974.

Erickson, Rita. "Characteristics of New Jersey Quilts, 1777-1867." In *What's American about American Quilts?* Washington, D.C.: Smithsonian Institution, National Museum of American History, 1995.

Finley, Ruth. *Old Patchwork Quilts and the Women Who Made Them*. Newton Centre, MA: Charles T. Branford Co., 1970. Originally published in 1929.

Fischer, Roger A. *Tippecanoe and Trinkets Too: The Material Culture of American Presidential Campaigns, 1828-1984*. Chicago: University of Illinois Press, 1988.

Fox, Sandi. *Small Endearments*. 2nd ed. Nashville: Rutledge Hill Press, 1994.

Garoutte, Sally. "Early Colonial Quilts in a Bedding Context." In *Uncoverings 1980: Volume 1 of the Research*

Papers of the American Quilt Study Group. Edited by Sally Garoutte. Lincoln, NE: American Quilt Study Group, 1981.

Gunn, Virginia. "Crazy Quilts and Outline Quilts: Popular Responses to the Decorative Art/Art Needlework Movement, 1876-1893." In *Uncoverings 1984: Volume 5*. Edited by Sally Garoutte. Lincoln, NE: American Quilt Study Group, 1985.

———. "Victorian Silk Template Patchwork in American Periodicals 1850-1875." In *Uncoverings 1983: Volume 4*. Edited by Sally Garoutte. Lincoln, NE: American Quilt Study Group, 1984.

Hall, Carrie A. and Rose Kretsinger. *Romance of the Patchwork Quilt*. San Francisco: Bonanza Books, 1935.

Hartley, Florence. *Ladies' Hand Book of Fancy and Ornamental Work*. Philadelphia: J. W. Bradley, 1861. (Original edition 1859).

Jenkins, Susan and Linda Seward. *The American Quilt Story: The How-To and Heritage of a Craft Tradition*. Emmaus, PA: Rodale Press, 1991.

Lane, Rose Wilder. *Woman's Day Book of American Needlework*. New York: Fireside/Simon Schuster, 1963.

Leman, Bonnie and Judy Martin. *Log Cabin Quilts*. Denver: Moon Over the Mountain Publishing/Leman Publications, 1980.

McCabe, James D. *The Illustrated History of the Centennial Exhibition*. Philadelphia: National Publishing Co., 1975.

McCall's Needlework and Crafts Editors. *McCall's Needlework & Crafts Bicentennial Quilt Book*. New York: McCall Pattern Co., 1975.

McMorris, Penny. *Crazy Quilts*. New York: Dutton Studio Books, 1984.

McMorris, Penny and Michael Kile. *The Art Quilt*. San Francisco: Quilt Digest Press, 1986. Published in conjunction with the exhibition "The Art Quilt" shown at the Los Angeles Municipal Art Gallery and other venues in 1986.

Montano, Judith Baker. *Art & Inspirations*. Concord, CA: C&T Publishing, 1997.

———. *The Crazy Quilt Handbook*. Concord, CA: C&T Publishing, 1986.

———. *Crazy Quilt Odyssey*. Concord, CA: C&T Publishing, 1991.

Noma, Seiroku. *Japanese Costume and Textile Arts*. Tokyo and New York: Weatherhill/Heibonsha, 1977.

Otto, Beatrice. *Fools Are Everywhere: The Court Jester Around the World*. Chicago: University of Chicago Press, 2001.

Peck, Amelia. *American Quilts & Coverlets in The Metropolitan Museum of Art*. New York: Dutton Studio Books, 1990.

Powell, G. Julie. *The Fabric of Persuasion: Two Hundred Years of Political Quilts*. Chadds Ford, PA: Brandywine River Museum, 2000.

Ramsey, Bets and Merikay Waldvogel. *Southern Quilts: Surviving Relics of the Civil War*. Nashville: Rutledge Press, 1997.

Reich, Sue. *Quilting News of Yesteryear: Crazy as a Bed-Quilt*. Lancaster, PA: Schiffer Books, 2006.

Robertson, Elizabeth Wells. *American Quilts*. New York: Studio Publications, 1948.

Safford, Carleton and Robert Bishop. *America's Quilts and Coverlets*. New York: E. P. Dutton, 1972.

Shaw, Robert. "Five Decades of Unconventional Quilts: The 1980s." Essay online. Available at http://www.roberteshaw.com/1980s.html.

Weissman, Judith Reiter and Wendy Lavitt. *Labors of Love: America's Textiles and Needlework, 1650–1930*. Avenel, NJ: Wings Books, 1987.

Zegart, Shelly. *American Quilt Collections: Antique Quilt Masterpieces*. Nashville: Rutledge Hill Press, 1998.

ADDITIONAL RESOURCES

Adamson, Jeremy. *Calico & Chintz: Antique Quilts from the Collection of Patricia S. Smith*. Washington, D.C.: Smithsonian Institution, 1997. A good introduction to pre-1850 textile trends and quilt styles.

Angotti, Charlotte. *Still Crazy After All These Quilts*. Santa Monica, CA: ME Publications, 1994.

Baranowski, Willa. *Historical Penny Squares Embroidery Patterns*. Paducah, KY: American Quilter's Society, 1996.

Baumgard, Toni. *Robert's Quilt: A Redwork Journey*. N.p.: Toni Baumgard, 2002.

Bond, Dorothy. *Crazy Quilt Stitches*. Cottage Grove, OR: Dorothy Bond, 1981.

Brick, Cindy. *The Stitcher's Language of Flowers*. Castle Rock, CO: Brickworks Press, 2003. Meanings for hundreds of flowers compiled from a variety of sources dating to the early 1800s into one comprehensive book. Also includes meanings of different herbs, trees, and even fruit and nuts.

———. "A Very Special Quilt," In *Crazy Quilt Society Newsletter*, Spring 1998. Additional information about the Maryland Kaleidoscope quilt.

Bridgeman, Cunningham. "The Making of the Mikado." In *Gilbert and Sullivan and Their Operas*. François Cellier and Cunningham Bridgeman. New York: Little, Brown and Company, 1914.

Cogdill, Sharon. "Imperialism, Racism and Ethnic Bigotry and Putting on a Performance of the Mikado." Research paper, St. Cloud State University, 1998. Available at http://condor.stcloudstate.edu/~scogdill/ mikado/racism.html.

Collins, Herbert R. *Threads of History: Americana Recorded on Cloth, 1775 To the Present*. Washington, D.C.: Smithsonian, 1979. Referenced in Robert A. Fischer's *Tippecanoe and Trinkets, Too*, this book contains more information about textile promotional items from political campaigns.

Cozart, Dorothy. "When the Smoke Cleared." In *The Quilt Digest #5*. San Francisco: Quilt Digest Press, 1987. This excellent article is one of the best sources of information on smoking-related ephemera, which includes cigarette or tobacco silks.

Crazy Quilt Society. *The Crazy Quilt Society*. Organization Web site. http://www.crazyquilt.com.

Crazy Quilt Stitches Pocket Guide. Little Rock, AR: Leisure Arts, n.d.

Dabbs, Christine. *Crazy Quilting: Heirloom Quilts; Traditional Motifs and Decorative Stitches*. Nashville: Rutledge Hill Press, 2000.

Delpiano, Robert. "Commedia Dell'Arte (Italian Comedy): Arlecchino (Harlequin, Arlechino, Arlequin)." Article online. http://www.delpiano.com/carnival/html/harlequin.html.

Dettore, Arlene and Beverly Maxvill. *Victorian Patchwork & Quilting*. New York: Meredith Press, 1995.

Doak, Carol. *Easy Machine Paper Piecing*. Woodinville, WA: That Patchwork Place, 1994.

Eha, Nancy. *Off the Beadin' Patch*. Stillwater, MN: Creative Visions Press, 1999.

Eichorn, Rosemary. *The Art of Fabric Collage: An Easy Introduction to Creative Sewing*. Newtown, CT: Taunton Press, 2003.

Ellmann, Richard. *Oscar Wilde*. New York: Alfred A. Knopf, 1988.

Embroiderers' Guild of America (EGA). Organization Web site. http://www.egausa.org/

Fons, Marianne, and Liz Porter. *The Quilter's Complete Guide*. Little Rock, AR: Leisure Arts, 1993.

Haigh, Janet. *Crazy Patchwork*. Chicago: Contemporary Publishing Group, 1998.

Hall, Jane. *Experts' Guide to Foundation Piecing*. Concord, CA: C&T Publishing, 2006.

———. "Log Cabin Quilts: Inspirations From the Past." Article online. Available at www.womenfolk.com/quilt_pattern_history/logcabin.htm.

Hall, Jane and Dixie Haywood. *Hall & Haywood's Foundation Quilts: Building On the Past*. Paducah, KY: American Quilter's Society, 2000.

Harding, Deborah. *Red & White: American Redwork Quilts*. 2 vols. New York: Rizzoli, 2000. Information on the advertisement's role in pattern motifs, as well as discussions on catalog sources and Redwork viewpoint.

Haywood, Dixie. *Contemporary Crazy Quilt Project Book*. New York: Crown Publishing, 1977.

———. *Crazy Quilt Patchwork: A Quick & Easy Approach*. New York: Dover Publications, 1986.

Heritage Search of the Quilters' Guild. *Quilt Treasures of Great Britain*. Nashville: Rutledge Hill Press, 1995. Contains an entire chapter devoted to sailor-made quilts, as well as other military quilts (also called soldiers' quilts).

Hiner, N. Ray and Joseph M. Hawes, eds. *Growing Up in America: Children in Historical Perspective*. Urbana: University of Illinois Press, 1985.

Laufer, Geraldine Adamich. *Tussie-Mussies: The Language of Flowers*. New York: Workman Publishing, 1993.

Larsdatter, Karen. "Foolish Clothing: Depictions of Jesters and Fools in Medieval and Renaissance Art." Article online. Available at www.larsdatter.com/foolwear.htm.

Leone, Diana. *Crazy With Cotton: Piecing Together Memories & Themes*. Concord, CA: C&T Publishing, 1996.

McKinnon, Gloria. *Creative Silk Ribbon Embroidery*. Hamilton, Australia: Creative House, 2003.

Michler, J. Marsha. *The Magic of Crazy Quilting: A Complete Resource for Embellished Quilting*. Iola, WI: Krause Publications, 1998.

Montano, Judith Baker. *The Art of Silk Ribbon Embroidery*. Concord, CA: C&T Publishing, 1993.

———. *Elegant Stitches: An Illustrated Stitch Guide & Source Book of Inspiration*. Concord, CA: C&T Publishing, 1995.

———. *Floral Stitches: An Illustrated Guide to Floral Stitchery*. Concord, CA: C&T Publishing, 2000.

"News." In *Quilter's Newsletter Magazine*, June 1998. Additional information about the Maryland Kaleidoscope quilt.

O'Brien, Ellen and Lyle Benedict. "19th and 20th Century: Infant and Childhood Mortality." In *Deaths, Disturbances, Disasters and Disorders in Chicago* (bibliography and article online). Available at www.chipublib.org/004chicago/disasters/infant_mortality.html.

Ortakales, Denise. "Children's Book Illustrators: Kate Greenaway (1846–1901)." Article online. Available at http://www.ortakales.com/illustrators/Greenaway.html.

Randle, Barbara. *Crazy Quilting With Attitude*. Iola, WI: Krause Publications, 2003.

———. *More Crazy Quilting With Attitude*. Iola, WI: Krause Publications, 2005.

Samples, Carole K. *Treasury of Crazy Quilt Stitches*. Paducah: KY: American Quilter's Society, 1999.

Smith. *Crazy Quilt Central*. Web site. http://www.geocities.com/SoHo/Lofts/6531/index.html

Stark, Dee. *A Spiderweb for Luck: Symbols & Motifs Used in Crazy Quilting*. Guilderland, NY: Victorian Handcrafts, 2003.

Twigg, Phyllis. *Victorian Redwork Sampler Quilt, c. 1895: 54 Patterns*. Annapolis, MD: Phyllis Twigg, 1999.

Williams, Charlotte Allen. *Florida Quilts*. Gainesville: University Press of Florida, 1992. Contains details about the Cross of St. Andrew quilt, a Crazy-style quilt made in Merced County, Pennsylvania, in 1835.

INDEX

ABOUT THE AUTHOR

Cindy Brick is an editor, designer, and writer who travels the world teaching about quilting and quilt history. A former editor for *Quilter's Newsletter*, she is also an American Quilter's Society–certified textiles appraiser and professional quilt restorer. She has written more than a hundred magazine articles and four books, including *Hanky-Panky Crazy Quilts*, *The Stitcher's Language of Flowers*, and the *Fabric Dating Kit*. Her next book, *Hanky Panky with a Flourish*, will also be released in 2008. She contributed to nearly all of *Encyclopaedia Britannica*'s quilt-related entries; she also consulted for three television specials on quilting (appeared in person on one) and was on *Simply Quilts* to explain her Hanky Panky quilt method. She is the "Old Things Considered" columnist for *McCall's Vintage Quilts* and a frequent contributor to other magazines, newsletters, and online listservs.

Cindy lives and works in Castle Rock, Colorado, with her family and two spoiled Weimaraners. For more on Cindy and quilt history, and for freebies (everything from screensavers to quilting, knitting, and crochet patterns), articles, and helpful tips, visit Cindy's company, Brickworks, at www.cindybrick.com or www.classygirlquilts.com, or call toll free: 1-888-48-BRICK.

"Fancy Illustrated Quilt" | Date: 1888 | Maker: Elizabeth Waller | Size: 60" x 72"

The amazing center panel of this quilt features an appliquéd design of the 1886 Saint Paul Winter Carnival Ice Palace. Twenty blocks surround it, each with motifs in appliqué or embroidery depicting people, the White House, flowers, birds, and more. The outer wide velvet border is edged in silk ball trim. Heavy trims and gimp braid—the kind we would think of today for trimming curtains, upholstery, or pillows—were a favorite for finishing Victorian-era Crazy quilts. Unfortunately, those trims usually wore out quickly, and were removed. Elizabeth outlived the completion of her quilt by less than a decade; she died in 1896. (Minnesota Historical Society)